# WORKING WITH MEN

### Edited by

## Tim Newburn and George Mair

## Russell House Publishing Ltd

*First published in 1996 by*

Russell House Publishing Limited
38 Silver Street
Lyme Regis
Dorset
DT7 3HS

**British Library Cataloguing-in-Publication Data:**
A catalogue record for this book is available from the British
Library.

ISBN: 1-898924-70-8

*Typeset by:*  Ed Skelly

*Printed by:*  Hobbs the Printers,
Totton, Hampshire.

# Working With Men

## Edited by Tim Newburn and George Mair

### Contents

# Contributors

**Karen Buckley** is a senior probation officer in Nottinghamshire who also writes and lectures on masculinity and sexuality. **Karen Young** completed an MA in Social Work at Nottingham University in 1988. Since then she has worked as a probation officer for Merseyside Probation Service. Her present specialist role is car crime co-ordinator. Karen has been actively involved with *Women In NAPO*, initially as NAPO anti-sexism officer, and more recently has helped to co-ordinate a national *Women in NAPO* conference.

**Andrew Cooper** is Professor of Social Work, Tavistock Clinic/University of East London and **Steve Trevillion** is Head of Department for Social Work at Brunel University College, Twickenham Campus, 300 St Margaret's Road, Twickenham, Middlesex, TW1 1PT.

**Luke Daniels** has trained in co-counselling and has been counselling men for over ten years. He has been working with men and violence for five years and has counselled hundreds of men in this time. His work with violent men has been documented in 'Pulling the Punches' a production for the Short Stories series on Channel 4. He also works as youth counsellor at a secondary school in London. More recently has has co-ordinated the first Black Fathers' Project in the UK and has started development work on a project for perpetrators of domestic violence and their partners for the London Borough of Sutton. He has worked as a trainer and consultant concerning domestic violence and has spoken at conferences and run workshops throughout Britain. He also has experience in the mental health field and has spoken at conferences on black people and mental health. He is a single parent and a writer.

**David Gardiner** is an Assistant Chief Probation Officer with Northumbria Probation Service, and was formerly Senior Probation Officer for the Intensive Probation Unit in its first three years of operation. **Don Nesbit** is a Probation Officer with the IPU. Both authors can be contacted via Northumbria Probation Service.

**Trefor Lloyd** has been involved in developing work with men since 1982. He has trained groups of youth workers, teachers, managers, social workers and prison officers. He is the author of numerous publications in this area and is a Director of *The B Team* and *Working With Men*. He, and these organisations, can be contacted at 320 Commercial Way, London SE15 1QN (1071 732 0409).

**Jane Mardon** is a member of Bishop Auckland College staff and is employed at Deerbolt YOI, Co. Durham as Deputy Education Co-ordinator and Head of Basic Skills. She has been working there with young male prisoners since 1981 and started the parenthood course in 1985. She has run workshops for the Trust for the Study of Adolescence and for ISTD on the topic of fathering and has written numerous articles on the subject. She can be contacted via HMYOI Deerbolt, Bowes Road, Barnard Castle, County Durham DL12 9BG.

**Dave Morran** has been joint co-ordinator of CHANGE since it was set up in 1989 to run a probation based groupwork programme for convicted male domestic violence offenders, the first of its type in the UK. In the past he has worked as a social worker in Glasgow, in Scottish prisons, and also with SACRO, the Scottish Association for the Care and Resettlement of Offenders. His interests in working with men as offenders and offenders as men is longstanding. Dave Morran now lectures in social work and criminal justice at the University of Stirling, and also acts as a consultant in work relating to masculinity and offending, and male domestic violence. He is co-author of a practitioners' handbook for probation-based work with men who are violent to partners, (forthcoming). He can be contacted at the University of Stirling, 01786 – 473171.

**Kevin Murphy** is a Probation Officer employed by the Inner London Probation Service and based at Camberwell Probation Centre. He has been involved in developing and running groups exploring male socialisation and offending. These have been held at probation centres, in prison, and at a day programme for drug users. A handbook giving details of all the sessions of the Men and Offending Group is being prepared and should be available by the end of 1995. Anyone who is interested in the Handbook, or would like to discuss the groups, should contact Kevin Murphy at Camberwell Probation Centre, 123 Grove Park, London SE5 8LB. (0171 733 0972).

# CHAPTER 1

# INTRODUCTION: WORKING WITH MEN

## Tim Newburn and George Mair

### Background

The title of this book gives, we hope, a good indication of the subject matter inside. It is a book that is written by, and written for, people working with men. More specifically, it is written by people working with men with the aim of changing them. What they seek to change varies, depending upon the focus of the work, though all the contributors, and many of the readers we expect, are involved in the business of helping men to change the way they behave. The primary focus of the book is 'offending' or 'criminal' behaviour. Violence, especially domestic violence, dominates, though a variety of other forms of offending, such as theft of and from cars, are also dealt with in some detail. Why, then, this book?

First, let us consider the nature of criminal activity. According to official Home Office statistics there were over 1.7 million offenders found guilty or cautioned (where guilt was admitted) for offences in England and Wales in 1994. Of these, over four fifths were men. The proportion would be even higher if the focus were solely on 'serious' or violent crimes. Crime, then, is predominantly a male activity. Indeed, given that one third of men in the UK will have a conviction for a serious offence by the age of 31 (Home Office Statistical Department, 1985) and even more will have taken part but not been convicted, we might even argue that being male almost inevitably involves some criminality. Of course, we have known about this association for a long time. It is nothing new. The vast overrepresentation of men in crime not only holds steady over time, but is also visible across the world. We are not alone in this. Crime is a universal male language. Until recently, however, there was little attempt to explore what it was about being a man that led to this overrepresentation (though see Newburn and Stanko (1994) for a number of essays on this question).

The second thing to consider is the response of statutory and voluntary agencies to all this criminal activity. Because of their overrepresentation in offending, men are also the major client group of all criminal justice professionals: police officers, probation officers, prison officers and other prison staff. Thus, for example, of the 41,700 people who commenced probation supervision in 1993, 84 per cent were men (Home Office, 1993). Of the 47,700 who commenced Community Service Orders 94 per cent were men, and of the 9,200 who commenced combination orders 92 per cent were men. Most starkly of all, of the 58,500 offenders who received custodial sentences in 1993, 96 per cent were men. As we say, no one who is at all familiar with criminal justice should be surprised by such figures. Everybody should, however, be concerned. Why should it be the case that such a high proportion of men receive criminal convictions (one third by their thirties) compared with women (one seventh by their thirties)?

The greatest surprise in all this is that so few people have paid attention to the fact that men are overrepresented in this way. Until relatively recently this was particularly evident in academic writing on the subject. In the last few years there has, however, developed within sociology, criminology, social work and related disciplines a growing awareness of the importance of the issue of 'masculinity' in understanding the circumstances and behaviour of men. As a result, a large amount of mainly academic literature has grown. Moreover, the practice of those professionals working with male offenders has begun to change. This book draws on this growing understanding and awareness of the subject of masculinity and, using examples of positive new developments in practice, aims to provide a guide for probation officers, social workers and others working in this field, to new ways of working with men who exhibit difficult, challenging and often aggressive or violent behaviour.

The probation service, social services and organisations in the voluntary sector are becoming increasingly interested in the whole subject of masculinity, and there now exists a number of specialist projects, within individual agencies, focusing on work with men. On the surface, it sounds somewhat odd to talk about working with men as if this were new to the probation service and social services. However, what is at issue is a reorientation of practice. Taking the probation service as an example, male clients of the probation service have hitherto tended to be perceived simply as offenders and worked with as such. There is now a gathering movement which recognises that it is at least as important to deal with these offenders as men as it is to deal with these men as offenders.

What the contributors to this book endeavour to do is to outline the rationale for, and the content of some of their work with, men. Not all are criminal justice professionals or, indeed, even work within criminal justice. What they all share, however, is a focus on the aspects of being a man that either result in considerable distress for others, and an increased likelihood of contact with the criminal justice system (violence, theft), or other characteristics associated with people most likely to become tangled up in the criminal justice system (poor parenting, alcohol and drug use).

The central aim of the book is to introduce those interested in developing new approaches to working with male offenders to a variety of styles, techniques, approaches, different focuses and contexts in which such practice can take place. None of the contributions is a style guide to how things *must* be done. The aim in each is to give a flavour of the work that has been undertaken, how it is delivered, the difficulties and dangers associated with it, together with an indication of what it can achieve. We hope in bringing these contributions together that the book will help stimulate further innovative work in these areas and that by introducing people working in these fields to each other that new networks for supporting and encouraging work with men and masculinity will develop. Moreover, through such networking and sharing of ideas, the hope is that the somewhat ad hoc and reactive nature of much of the current work with men will develop a more solid focus.

### Angry Men

Although we have suggested that work that specifically focuses on masculinity has a relatively short history, the first chapter in this volume describes work that was conducted over a decade ago. Andrew Cooper and Stephen Trevillion in reflecting on their work with 'angry men' argue that the work they did then has continuing relevance and resonance now. In their everyday practice the two authors, and other male workers in their inner city patch-based office, were confronted by a group of men who made very forceful demands on the staff of the office. Interestingly, and perhaps not surprisingly, the authors acknowledge that in some respects they drifted into an awareness of masculinity as an issue. Thus, although the issues being confronted are, in many respects, similar to those identified in subsequent chapters, there is a feeling in this case that the workers were very much forced to make it up as they went along.

The clients described by Cooper and Trevillion all inhabited crisis-ridden existences. The material demands that they made for money and accommodation, for example, simply could not be met and significant questions therefore arose as to what could be offered and whether any difference could be made to their lives? They exhibited destructive tendencies, threatened violence both to themselves and to their workers. They felt persecuted and persecuted others in turn. Working with them, therefore, was marked by a struggle; a struggle which led almost inevitably to crisis which, at least in part, resolved the tension between worker and client which existed. Central to the success of this work was the strength and survival of the worker himself. The masculine pronoun is carefully chosen here, for in every case the worker was male, and questions are inevitably raised as to whether female workers could or would have chosen to work in such a way. This 'confrontational' approach to problem-solving is in its own way a highly masculine form and is significantly different from the other programmes described here, many of which explicitly eschewed confrontation.

### Modular therapy

By contrast, the work described by David Gardiner and Don Nesbit is in some respects, of necessity, significantly more structured in its approach. Once again, in part, the work with men was arrived at largely as a result of experience of practice rather than theory. They describe the background to, and a number of the modules in, an intensive probation programme run by Northumbria Probation Service. The approach adopted was based on cognitive behavioural therapy. This revolves around the assumption – stated crudely – that the ways in which people think set limitations on the ways in which they behave and that, consequently, changes in behaviour can most effectively be brought about by altering their ways of thinking. Participation on the course was voluntary, in the main, and the courses themselves were short and intensive, rarely lasting beyond a few days but being full-time for that period.

The authors describe two of the modules in detail. The first, an anger management course called 'keeping your head'; the second, entitled 'relationships for men', focused on abusive relationships. They found that although men were willing to acknowledge violence to themselves and to other men, they were much less willing to do so in relation to women and children. One of the key issues raised again in this chapter is the gender of the staff and, more particularly in this case, whether mixed gender staffing would have been appropriate. They offer no clear guidance on this, but are clear that a mixed gender clientele – which they tried – is unlikely to work satisfactorily.

### Motor offenders

Theft of, or from, cars is one of the most common offences in the UK. It is widely recognised that young offenders are responsible for much of this crime but, as Karen Buckley and Karen Young remind us, it is all too often ignored that it is young *male* offenders who predominate. Buckley and Young argue that it is important to bring masculinity into the frame when dealing with motor offenders, and describe the elements of a project for such offenders based in Merseyside – the Car Offenders Project (COP). The project is available to the courts for those convicted of serious car-related crimes as a condition added to a probation order.

Buckley and Young raise some interesting issues about the structure and content of COP which are worth emphasising. First, although there is a focus on masculinity and the great majority of offenders are male, females are not barred from the project. A few women have attended and completed the project, although the importance of having female workers is stressed. Second, there is the thorny question of how far motor projects should go in catering to the desire for thrills of motor offenders. The COP initially offered go-karting, but after various problems this component of the programme has been dropped and replaced by an 'image of the car' session. The need for flexibility is a key aspect of dealing with this group of offenders.

## Men and offending

A second probation-based project is described by Kevin
Murphy. These 'men and offending' groups were run as part of
a conditional requirement added to a probation order; the
referral basis being similar to the motor project described later
by Karen Buckley and Karen Young. The programme contains
twelve sessions which range in their focus from looking at the
expectations on men, the process of becoming a man, to an
examination of the benefits and costs of offending and
challenges to racism and sexism. Murphy describes three of the
sessions in detail: 'what are men expected to be?'; 'when did I
become a man?'; and a session taking the focus on transitions
to manhood one step forward, and looking at the idea of
'proving' oneself as a man. One of the characteristics which
distinguishes this work from some of the other programmes
described in this volume is its more general focus. That is, it
does not have a highly specific target group such as spouse
abusers or motor vehicle offenders, for example. Rather, the
focus is on 'persistent' male offenders. The focus is upon
masculinity as it impinges on offending behaviour.

One of the issues alluded to by Murphy, and by several of the
other contributors, is the role of evaluation or research. The
innovative character of much of the practice described in this
volume means that it is of particular importance that the work
is observed and 'evaluated' by outsiders. Ideally, of course,
research would begin at the very outset of new projects and
would use a variety of techniques to assess the impact of the
work. In general, the reality is that rather more limited
evaluations are more likely to be undertaken. Sometimes,
because of limited resources, these can often involve little
more than crude indicators of user satisfaction. It would be
surprising if an introduction like this, written by two
researchers, did not include a plea for more, and more
rigorous, research. Although we have an obvious interest to
declare here, we are firmly of the opinion that innovative
practice with offenders deserves proper, rigorous scrutiny.

## Men's violence to women

Luke Daniels, describing in detail the programme he has run at
the Everyman Centre in Brixton, focuses mainly on men's
violence to women. His context, however, is not criminal
justice. Clients for the Everyman Centre have generally come

as self-referrals, the men hearing of the Centre via GPs, citizens' advice bureaux, the police or just by word of mouth. Indeed, during the night after the screening of a television programme about the counselling programme the Centre received over 500 inquiries about its work. Although the Centre now takes some referrals from the probation service, the bulk of the work remains unconnected with formal criminal justice. Luke Daniels describes his approach as being loosely based on co-counselling, but adapted as a result of many years of work with violent men. In practice, the six month course is half one-to-one counselling and half groupwork. Clearly, the second element is much closer to the work undertaken by Kevin Murphy, for example, though there are also some significant differences. The co-counselling approach, he argues, allows the men to receive counselling, it serves to raise their general awareness both of themselves and of some key issues around their masculinity, and helps them develop some basic counselling skills of their own. The subjects covered in the groupwork include many common to other programmes such as racism, sexism and homophobia, as well as others such as the meaning of love and parenting – the latter being an often neglected subject which we return to below.

### CHANGE programme

One of the issues Daniels raises, as someone with much experience of working with men for change, is the sceptical view of such work that is often, and understandably, held by feminists. This concern is also found in David Morran's chapter on the CHANGE programme for men who are violent to their partners. As Morran argues, there may be some dangers in the work with violent men polarising into two camps: the largely 'respectable' work with convicted offenders that takes place post-court (such as his own), and the work taking place largely outside the criminal justice system with men who *merely* acknowledge a problem of violence (closer to the work described by Luke Daniels). Morran's concern, and one we share, is that by confining work with violent men to the criminal justice context, only a small minority of men who employ violence in their relationships will be reached.

As with other projects described here, the CHANGE programme had strict assessment criteria for determining the suitability of potential clients. This included the commitment of the man to attending the programme, levels of drug and alcohol use and, crucially, the safety of the woman to whom the man had been violent. About one third of potential clients are rejected for lacking motivation or denying responsibility and, as Morran acknowledges, there is no clear pattern as to what happens to these men, the courts varying significantly in the way they view domestic violence. Given what has already been noted above about the relative absence of voluntary groups working in this area, there is obviously one further important question that remains about what happens to the men who are rejected as unsuitable by such a project. How is their violence to be confronted?

## *Parenting*

One of the places in which a violent and highly masculinised self-image is unlikely to be challenged is in prison. Indeed, this is perhaps the context in which there is the most pressing need for work around masculinity to be developed. The penultimate chapter in the collection, by Jane Mardon, looks at a prison-based programme, albeit not one predicated primarily or explicitly on masculinity. Her work, and that of her colleagues, in Deerbolt Young Offender Institution has a much more tightly focused subject – parenting. Anyone who has spent much time in a YOI talking to the young men there about their lives will have been struck by how many of them are, or are soon to become, fathers (seemingly about one third of the inmates at Deerbolt). As Jane Mardon argues, many of these young men are looking to bring up their children in ways that are qualitatively different from the ways in which they were brought up. Their lack of education and 'poor social and life skills' make it likely that this will be a struggle for them.

The course at Deerbolt covers both the practical side and, crucially for young men, the emotional side of childcare. It looks at childbirth, at building and sustaining relationships with children and partners, with health and safety and first aid, with family planning and STDs, and issues such as child abuse and the financial circumstances of young families. Though the term 'masculinity' is used less often in this work than in many of the other programmes discussed, it is clearly at least as central. Families, of course, are perhaps the most significant domain in which masculinities are established. Relationships between boys and their fathers (or where these are absent) and, perhaps even more crucially, relationships between boys and their mothers, have life-long effects. Of course, families are far from stable units. Jane Mardon points out one further subject, the role of step-parents, that receives much superficial coverage in the tabloid press, but is often not confronted very constructively elsewhere. All relationships with parent figures, 'natural' parents or not, are central to an understanding of male self-identity. Becoming a caring partner and parent is something most people wish to be, and yet it doesn't come easily. As one of the participants in the Deerbolt Parenthood Group commented: "I had a terrible relationship with my father and even now I don't ever want to see him again. I don't want my baby to feel like that about me. The course helps you to handle things like that".

## *Training*

Although the type of work with men described in this volume has a relatively short history and is still in its infancy, two of the organisations that have played a significant part in its development – *Working With Men* and *The B Team* – are mentioned by more than one of the contributors. One of the mainstays of both organisations, Trefor Lloyd, discusses the role of training in the final essay in the book. Lloyd starts from and recasts many of the issues raised in the preceding papers. Just as all the contributors are circumspect in their claims for their work, Trefor Lloyd, discussing the role of training in the development of work with men, is careful to point to what it can't achieve before turning to its potential.

In particular, Lloyd counsels against having too many or too high expectations of training. In many ways training begins as, and can help with, personal development. However, it can be hard to follow-up such an approach with other more focused work in other areas. There is some indication, he implies, that interest in the whole area of masculinity and working with men may be running ahead of the ability to work in this area. The claims for the training in this area have been overinflated and this has been allowed to happen, Lloyd argues, partly because of a lack of understanding on the part of 'management' of the issues involved, and partly because of a lack of material which focuses on and tackles practice issues. A practice-based approach is what is most likely to raise practitioners' confidence and enable them to develop new work. Indeed, this is the rationale behind this volume. It is to provide a forum for those involved in innovative work with men to describe what they do and the potential and pitfalls of such work.

## Conclusion

We hope that readers will feel that such work has much
potential and that there is much that can be developed out of
the approaches described here. It is not going to be easy, of
course. Whilst not wishing to conclude this introduction on a
downbeat note, it is important to recognise that one of the
things that links almost all the work described in this volume is
the difficult circumstances under which it takes or took place.
David Morran describes much of his work experience in this
area as 'hard, often depressing and quite isolating. Operating
in a culture where there is little tangible support for men to
challenge or change their 'lifestyles', as may be present in parts
of the US, Canada or Australia, can lead to feelings not only
that one is often struggling in the work with individual men,
but that the work itself has little cultural approval and, in the
face of the often understandable mistrust of some women's
groups, and an uncertain political climate, little opportunity
for future funding'. Nonetheless, under such circumstances
innovative and challenging work with men has developed and
continues to take place. As it continues, so the cultural
resistance to it will diminish. The pace at which this process of
change takes place can only speed up, however, if proper
financial support for such work is made available.

## References

Home Office. (1993) *Probation Statistics England and Wales*,
London: Home Office.

Home Office Statistical Department. (1985) *Criminal Careers
of those born in 1953, 1958, 1963*, Statistical Bulletin No. 5/85,
London: Home Office Statistical Department.

Newburn, T. and Stanko, E. A. (1994) *Just Boys Doing
Business? Men, masculinities and crime*, London: Routledge.

# CHAPTER 2

# SURVIVAL AND CHANGE: SOCIAL WORK WITH ANGRY MEN

## Andrew Cooper and Steven Trevillion

### Introduction

In this chapter we discuss the risk elements in encounters with six angry male clients of a social services neighbourhood team. Their preoccupation with basic survival needs produced an identification of the worker with an 'elusive stolen object'; this leads to a discussion of how we also felt we had become identified with an image of persecuting parent, rooted in their childhood experience. The key notion of our 'struggle' with them is linked to that of 'boundary-setting' and the therapeutic value of the characteristic escalation of client/worker conflict is examined. The worker's survival is seen as a confirmation of the client's personal integrity. The process of disengagement is then analysed with particular attention to the material transactions between client and worker that served to mark the end of the engagement. We acknowledge the minimalist nature of our strategy with these men, and attempt to examine outcomes.

### History

Most social workers have encountered a client who rejects everything offered, but continually returns for more. For both parties it seems to be a relationship of despair, controlled by feelings of rage, frustration, helplessness and guilt. Despite his rejection of us, the client seems hooked, and despite the hopelessness of it all, we sometimes become hooked ourselves. More often, perhaps, we give up.

This analysis of our work with a number of 'angry men' was originally published in 1985. Nevertheless, we believe it remains relevant in a number of ways. To begin with, the almost painful clarity that we both still have about our experiences with these men leads us to think that the piece dealt with some fundamental and enduring features of social work practice which make it relevant for a contemporary readership. Second, as people closely involved with preparing social work students for the world of work, we know that in the intervening years, social work itself has become a more dangerous profession. Conflict, confrontation and sometimes violence have become almost commonplace to an extent which few would have predicted in the 1980s. The reasons for this lie deep in the nature of contemporary welfare and include the scarcity of almost all those resources, including time, which make it possible to get alongside rather than argue with others. But whatever the reasons, it seems very unlikely that this trend towards conflict and confrontation will reverse itself in the short-term. More than ever before social workers need to work with anger and conflict and, insofar as our analysis offers a framework for understanding and managing anger, we believe it has a contribution to make. Community care policies, the increasing numbers of single homeless men, cuts in the real value of social security benefits and much else besides, mean that there is probably more anger around and more genuine need for this kind of work than ever before. However, social workers now find themselves operating in a very different legal and organisational environment than that of the early 1980s.

In the 1980s we saw ourselves as 'patch workers' offering a flexible service to any member of the local community who wanted help. We found ourselves working with these 'angry men' simply because they asked us for help. We did not have to and probably could not have justified our work in terms of a specific needs assessment or mental health assessment, let alone any process of care management. In a world dominated by targeting, value for money and decreasing professional autonomy, it may actually be much more difficult to justify engaging in this kind of work, which has few obvious outcomes and does not fit neatly into any of the standard ways in which contemporary social work activities are usually classified. Nevertheless, we remain convinced that such work is absolutely essential and to some extent inevitable. In this context spending time with angry men – even though it may not always be clear what is being achieved – is not only good, but is also cost effective social work practice.

## First impressions

This article arises from our experience of working in an inner-city, patch-based office, in a locality with a large migratory population attracted by the multitude of cheap hotels, hostels and bedsits. We began comparing notes on our contact with a number of such clients, and noticed some striking and unusual resemblances in the pattern of their transactions with us. These discussions took place against a background of awareness among team members of a loose grouping of male clients who periodically forced their attentions on us. They seemed to use our duty system on a haphazard but repeated basis, so that in the space of a few weeks most of the seven social workers in the team would have encountered them. They all made their impressions through extreme behaviour or the threat of it, sometimes confronting the team with severe management problems. Short of calling the police to remove these men from the building, attempts to control their invasive behaviour were largely thwarted. However, partly because the team had adopted unorthodox yardsticks of success and failure in an attempt to value short-term work with transient clients, we also felt we had helped some of the men. Indeed, given their habit of scorning all our attempts to be helpful, we began to see that their return visits to us signified some measure of success in itself. Closer examination revealed both a history of greater consistency of response from workers, and more clearly definable processes in the work than we had imagined.

We began to think more systematically about our work with these clients by selecting from memory half a dozen whom at least one of us knew well, and both of us had encountered on occasions. All were men, five between the ages of 25 and 35, and one in his mid-50s. All of them were single, and only one had any long-term roots in the neighbourhood. In spite of their reluctance to use traditional casework structures, five of them had been allocated a particular worker at some point in the history of their contact with the office. In retrospect, allocation to a specific worker appears to have been primarily an institutional defence against the disruptive impact these men had on the functioning of the duty system. Sometimes allocation served as a temporary holding operation, and in two cases it spanned the remainder of the period of work.

As for anyone living on supplementary benefit and in insecure housing, these clients' objective conditions of life were unacceptably poor. They emerged as a distinct group not least because personal deprivation seemed to have rendered them unable to make use of even the limited opportunities available to them. Nothing we say below is intended to imply that our work with them could act as a substitute for better material conditions of life.

### Early encounters

None of these men seemed to have a sound sense of relationship to either their past or future, and they told us few details of childhood experience or current aspirations. They appeared to inhabit a perpetually anguished or crisis-ridden present, and this obliged us to work almost exclusively in the here and now with these men. This lack of temporal context seemed to flow directly from their urgent preoccupation and anxiety about meeting basic survival needs. Five presented recurring housing or financial crises, and three communicated sexual desires powerfully, if sometimes obliquely. The urgency of their felt needs obliterated the possibility of using the social work relationship as a co-operative dialogue. Rather, they seemed to seize upon it as an opportunity to extract something from the agency, which was not only essential to survival, but which they also assumed we were maliciously withholding from them.

Early in our contact with Derek, for example, we made him a number of small payments to help him secure or retain accommodation. When a series of evictions and lost or stolen DSS giros led us to refuse to continue paying, the ferocity of his sense of injustice was startling. Similarly, when Albert's rather menacing sexual fantasies led women social workers to refuse to see him, there began a long engagement in which his sole preoccupation became the acquisition of a woman worker. These expressed needs were real enough, but in some unaccountable way we were made to feel that we had actually stolen the desired object from the client. In one exchange, Michael vehemently attacked a worker for the superior quality of his clothes. Derek repeatedly castigated one of us with accurate knowledge of our weekly wage and our extreme indolence in earning this money. They mounted a furious campaign against us for the return of the stolen object, but underlying this envy there seemed to be an identification of the worker as both thief and stolen object. In the person of the worker these men seemed to see the outline of that which they had lost.

## The worker as persecuting parent

Our impression is that all these clients had suffered real childhood trauma and deprivation, although this may have been elaborated on in fantasy. Derek spoke of having been abandoned by his mother at the age of two and "living in about 30 different foster homes". He once described the state as his parents. Albert had been in care, and sometimes likened the regime in our office to his persecuting childhood memories. We believe that at least two of the other men had been in care as children. Understandably, then, these clients seemed to assimilate social services departments and other welfare agencies to an image of a bad or cheating parent. As workers we felt that all these clients were in search of a 'lost' parent with a degree of desperation, even ferocity, to which ordinary concepts of transference hardly do justice. They expected to have to bully or manipulate us into giving tokens of love, but anything extracted in this way seemed irrevocably tainted by the manner in which it had been acquired. The real thing remained continually elusive. Derek's habit of losing or having his weekly giro stolen, and his evictions from successive hotels illustrated this, and echoed his account of his childhood. Typically, he returned time and again to the office demanding to be rescued from his predicament.

These four clients seemed to find their workers acutely persecuting. This usually reflected a generally conspiratorial view of the social world, bordering on the paranoid. For example, Michael likened us to his vivid fantasies of sadistic policemen, and Albert accused male workers of conspiring against him to deny him access to women workers. Feeling persecuted, they actively persecuted all those with whom they came in contact, including those who, unlike us, could have provided them with the material goods they sought. The destructive consequences of their own actions were ascribed to the inaccessibility of the desired object. "If only you would give me money, better housing, a woman social worker, none of these other dreadful things would have happened", they seemed to say. Apparently cut off from any sense of personal worth, they were also cut off from any sense of personal responsibility. Unbounded, unloved, out of control, they seemed to be careering through life damaging themselves and others, and demanding the impossible.

## The struggle

Contact with these clients occurred in a crisis-laden atmosphere. They sought out social workers at times when rage, frustration and despair of their own survival led them to demand rescue from the perceived injustices of the world. "If you do not help me in the way I want, I will die or kill myself, and it will be your fault", was the uncompromising message they gave us. Any attempt by the worker to exercise personal or professional autonomy led to conflict. Within the first few minutes the stage was set for what felt like a struggle for survival. As in a ritual combat, it felt as though one must live and the other die. This combat into which we were inexorably drawn was a product of these men's sado-masochistic vision of the world, in which it seemed that to punish or be punished were the only options.

All six men with whom we worked threatened violence to themselves or others, and sometimes acted it out. Michael took repeated overdoses of drugs between visits to the office, and indulged in graphic fantasies about nurses and brutalising policemen. He usually reacted with extreme verbal abuse when his requests for instant attention were denied. On one occasion Chris smashed a window in the interview room and pulled out a telephone lead, injuring his hand in the process. The worker has effectively to choose between provoking anger or self-mutilation on the one hand, or buying off the threat by capitulating to the client on the other. If the worker gives in, then from our experiece he or she is overwhelmed by feelings of exploitation and worthlessness. In the long run the client's anger seems less threatening than this sense of being rendered worthless.

Most of these men seemed to retain a minimal sense of the worker's capacity to survive their onslaught, and were able to return to the scene of the 'crime' and repeat it. There were two exceptions. Ron indecently exposed himself at two other local agencies and was perceived by us as extremely threatening, although he never made explicit threats. Perhaps both he and we recognised that he could not exercise even minimal control should he get in touch with his anger. He was never allocated a particular worker, and after he had ceased contact with the office we heard that he had attacked and injured several strangers with a knife. He is now in a special hospital. At the other extreme, Terry's defences against his own anger were so rigid that he could find no way of making contact with others. His polite, co-operative demeanour during a phase of allocated work belied a fierce split between his public and private selves. His anger was entirely turned in on himself, a fact to which his heavily scarred body bore witness. He simply faded away from the office, and all our attempts to engage with him failed.

These two men represent opposite extremes of the continuum and define the therapeutic territory occupied by our work with the core group of the other four, with whom the theme of struggle was ever-present in all our transactions, and left no room for those elements which one might take for granted in most social work relationships. Yet it proved a tool without which the work would either have been naive or dangerously masochistic. We came to recognise that the energy these clients injected into their struggles with us could become a force for positive change, if only we could obtain the right kind of therapeutic leverage. Like novices in the martial arts, we stumbled upon a method which used the attacking weight of the client against his own resistance to change.

### The process of escalation

Refusal to comply with his demands for rescue will inevitably escalate the client's sense of outrage and desperation. But capitulation will merely reinforce his fear that he cannot survive independently, and so with Chris, for example, one of us spent six months doing little else than saying "No". Escalation can have positive consequences. As we have suggested above, it is the worker's ability to survive which really interests the client, rather than the material tokens of survival he seeks to extract. Therefore demands for material help are best met by an offer of the worker's time, but the value of this time can only be preserved by limiting its availability, and requests for unscheduled meetings should be refused. This combination of messages, which could be described as 'positive refusal', will serve to place increasing emphasis on the boundary between the client and the worker. An alarming sequence of ever more angry and desperate demands will ensue, spiralling towards a critical point. In this phase of work we occasionally found no alternative but to call in the police when clients refused to leave the premises.

### The critical point

As the client repeatedly fails to destroy the boundary between the worker and himself, his awareness of its strength grows. It represents the sum total of all the energy he has used to try and destroy it. Eventually the worker becomes identified with the boundary, and at the peak of his anger the client attempts to symbolically annihilate both. Although we did not know it at the time, when Albert grabbed hold of one of us while attempting to invade private office space, when Chris smashed the office window, and when Derek and Michael mounted highly envious and aggressive verbal attacks on workers, they had reached a turning-point in their relationship to us. Each man's final assault was also a therapeutic crisis, a fulcrum which tipped him from despair into hope. The sheer strength of their attacks seemed to carry them over a threshold of change. Finally they internalised the boundary, and began to establish a more secure sense of self. They no longer saw themselves as partly contained within the worker, and embarked on a process of separation from the office marked by a progressive relaxation of the struggle.

By defending his or her boundaries, the worker has helped to confirm the personal integrity of the client, and increased his felt capacity for survival. All the energy in this therapeutic process comes from the client, who is arguably searching for some sense of self-worth in the only way he knows how.

### Disengagement and confirmation of identity

We were struck by the way in which several of the men registered some sort of completion of the work through reparative gestures. Derek requested help to find voluntary work with the elderly. On his last visit to the office Michael offered a pound towards the team's voluntary fund. Chris took to supplying the reception area with a variety of informative leaflets, and on one occasion a job lot of Playboy Club ashtrays. Ron's relationship with us ended on a sadder note, with requests from the hospital social worker that we locate a radio and some photographs he believed he had left in a local shop. Finally he asked the workers in the team to write to him in hospital. Although we felt we had given Ron very little, he evidently felt he had left something behind with us.

Some of the men also signified the closure of the work through another partly symbolic transaction, namely a request or series of requests that we provide them with a letter of identity. Although each client seemed to have a genuine need for such a document in order to cash a DHSS giro, the request invariably came in the phase of disengagement. This exchange of letters and reparative objects closely resembles that phase of early childhood in which the boundary between 'me' and 'not me' may be negotiated through transitional objects. Perhaps Ron's request that we forward him possessions he had left behind in the neighbourhood represented a dislocated version of this process. But sadly, we could find no trace of the articles he believed he had lost.

## Conclusions

In our experience these clients were unwilling or unable to progress to make use of other forms of social work help. This is frustrating for the worker, but perhaps the client will do the work elsewhere. The way in which these men disengaged and disappeared from view means that we have only limited evidence for longer term outcomes from the work. However, through contact with other offices we learned that Chris had found himself a job for a time and seemed to be managing his money better than before. Derek successfully negotiated a council tenancy for himself, and made contact with his mother in the United States. Albert has been doing some voluntary work with a local agency who previously found him almost unmanageable. So there is some slim evidence that the work empowered these men and increased their self-determination, but given their fragile sense of self at the outset the work may well have to be repeated at a later time.

We would like to stress that the method we have advocated above is not intended as a punishment for the good of the client, but as a means of transforming a potentially destructive process into a constructive outcome. It is because these men imposed themselves on us with a sort of blind necessity, while simultaneously rejecting all the usual gestures of help, that we adopted the minimalist strategy we have described. Surviving and setting boundaries was all that was possible and, we believe, all that the clients were really asking of us. In retrospect, only one of the clients discussed in this paper seems likely to have posed a threat of actual physical harm to us. But how does one distinguish the potentially dangerous client from the merely aggressive or angry one? We suggest first that due attention is given to any evidence of past violent behaviour towards people rather than objects. Second, we think it important to distinguish between a client who directly incorporates the person of the worker in violent fantasies, and one who appears to trust the worker with his violent feelings. Attacks on the worker's ability to help the client probably indicate some minimal awareness of the professional boundary separating self from other. However, should a worker be directly threatened with violence, we suggest the termination of work.

Provided a worker takes notice of these possible warning signs, we do not believe that the confrontational method suggested in this paper increases the risk of physical violence. Indeed, we think that in the long term it decreases the risk of violence, by helping at least some angry men to feel more in control of themselves and less persecuted by the outside world.

Whereas some therapies may actively seek to encourage the expression of aggressive feelings in order to promote a cathartic release of tension, our work has had quite different goals. We have been concerned to help a certain group of clients internalise a boundary between behaviour which is acceptable and that which is not, and in so doing to reinforce their precarious sense of self. 'Ventilationist' strategies have been criticised for promoting anti-social behaviour, but 'positive refusal' is highly judgemental of aggressive behaviour and has as one of its goals the resocialisation of some very anti-social people.

We remain unsure why all the clients in this group came to be allocated to male workers. Possibly there was a sexist dynamic at work in the team, resulting in male workers 'taking on' difficult, aggressive men clients. Similar factors could account for our lack of awareness of an equivalent group of women clients. On the other hand, gender identification may be a highly significant factor in work with this type of client.

As a team we became increasingly adept at identifying members of this group of clients early in their contact with us. Because we learned to define our expectations more realistically, we think we helped more of them more often, at less emotional cost to ourselves. Effective teamwork and a coherent duty system were essential to this process. Because these clients find it hard to use planned intervention, their initial contact with the agency is likely to take the form of a series of one-off appointments. For some it will never proceed beyond this, but the recognition that the client is embarking on a process with the agency rather than an individual worker must occur at a collective level. This is more difficult to achieve in an area office, where duty rotates among several different teams, than in a patch setting or area-based intake team.

In recommending that it is possible or desirable to undertake effective social work against such apparently long odds, we may be justifiably suspected of the same sado-masochistic tendencies we attribute to these clients. In response, we would say that we both experienced a sense of reward each time we completed and survived the work with one of these men. If, as a result, the clients experienced a similar reward, then we believe the work to have been worthwhile.

### References

Berkovitz, L. (1962) *Aggression: a Social Psychological Analysis*, McGraw-Hill: New York.

Berkovitz, L. (1973) 'The Case for Bottling up Rage' *New Society*, Vol. 25, 27/9/73.

Davis, H. (1984) 'Impossible Clients' *J. Social Work Practice*, Vol. 1, No. 2.

Freud, S. (1905): *Three Essays on Sexuality*, Pelican Freud Library, 1977, Penguin.

Hall, A. S. (1974): *The Point of Entry: a Study of Client Reception in the Social Services*, Allen & Unwin.

Klein, M. (1980): 'Envy and Gratitude', in *Envy and Gratitude and Other Works*, Hogarth Press and the Institute of Psychoanalysis.

Lacan, J. (1979): *The Four Fundamental Concepts of Psychoanalysis*, Penguin.

Menzies, I. (1960): 'A Case Study in the Functioning of Social Systems as a Defence Against Anxiety', *Human Relations Journal*, Vol. 13, No. 2.

Prins, H. (1975) 'A Danger to Themselves and Others', *British Journal of Social Work*, Vol. 5, No. 3.

Winnicott, D. W. (1965): *The Maturational Process and the Facilitating Environment*. Hogarth Press.

# CHAPTER 3

# COGNITIVE BEHAVIOURAL GROUPWORK WITH MALE OFFENDERS: THE NEWCASTLE UPON TYNE INTENSIVE PROBATION UNIT

**David Gardiner and Don Nesbit**

## Introduction

The Newcastle Intensive Probation Unit was set up in 1990 initially as one of a number of Home Office instigated, and very diverse, pilot projects. The initiative, as a whole, has been researched by the Home Office Research and Planning Unit[1]. The Newcastle Unit became a demonstration project in cognitive behavioural groupwork with offenders (both male and female) attracting national recognition. Its success has been due, we feel, partly to the content of its programmes (two of which are described in detail later in this chapter) but also to a series of key decisions and choices in the design of the project, to which we will turn first.

## The cognitive behavioural approach

The decision to adopt a cognitive behavioural approach to groupwork was made because of the growing interest at the time in this type of work, and our belief that it could have a considerable impact on offenders. Put simply, a cognitive behavioural approach challenges the ways people think and act, based on the premise that changes to how they think will bring about adaptations to their behaviour. Ross (1991)[2] usefully summarises the kinds of cognitive defects offenders may have, such as impulsiveness (not thinking before acting) and concrete (as opposed to abstract) thinking. These are characterised by an inability to understand the reasons for rules and laws or to consider the views of others. Some offenders have difficulties with conceptual rigidity, being inflexible and dogmatic, they become locked into cycles of dysfunctional behaviour. They may have poor levels of ability in relation to solving problems within relationships, through being unable to predict the consequences of their behaviour. Egocentricity is common, according to Ross, and is manifested in a lack of sensitivity to the thoughts and feelings of other people. Value systems may be very limited, often to a concept of, "if it's good for me it must be good". Finally, offenders might have trouble with critical reasoning, being irrational and illogical, they are easily influenced by others and rarely self-critical.

Our approaches to these issues will be discussed in detail elsewhere in this chapter. In the meantime, suffice it to say that we see the cognitive behavioural approach as being good common sense, practical and down to earth. It is a method of working that offenders can comprehend. As it is about thinking and acting rather than feeling, though feelings are frequently discussed in our work, we believe it to be less threatening than a more 'therapeutic' approach, perhaps especially for men

## Voluntary attendance

Voluntarism, as opposed to attendance imposed by courts, was another important choice made at the outset. There is, we believe, a place for conditional groups within probation practice, where the subject matter is directly offence related (drink driving for example) and where the seriousness of the offence warrants a Probation Order with extra strings attached. On the other hand, voluntary programmes attract a generally more motivated clientele and improve rather than diminish attendance levels (typical completion rates for Intensive Probation Unit 'courses' – the preferred term – are around 85 – 90 per cent). Voluntary groups can also cover a wide range of topics, i.e. they do not necessarily have to be offence focused. Also, offenders can come into a programme earlier in their criminal career and perhaps be diverted more readily from prolonging or escalating it. Nevertheless, the Unit also works with many high risk and highly convicted offenders; up to 40 per cent of our total referrals have previous custodial experience.

## A modular system

The choice of a modular approach, of 13 different self-standing but complementary courses, was important in allowing attenders, with their probation officers, to tailor an individualised, flexible package to their own needs. Some people who come to the Unit have completed one groupwork module, others six or seven. Course topics include car crime, anger management, drugs, alcohol, assertiveness, stress, relationships, offending behaviour, employment and gambling.

A vital decision in the design of the project was to run modules as three, four or five day full-time blocks rather than one short session per week over a longish period (perhaps the most usual format for groupwork in probation). As we were to be running a large number of groups per year, we felt it would be better for leaders to finish one before starting the next. The alternative was to have various modules running in parallel. We also believed offenders would get more from the intensive, full time format – it is easy to keep defences intact for a couple of hours once a week! We thought, and subsequent experience confirmed, that groups would form more effectively and get into serious work more readily when handled as short sharp blocks. On a practical level, as we were using a range of community based venues for our groupwork it was felt that booking rooms, transporting equipment and paying offenders' travelling expenses would be dealt with more economically and efficiently over a few days rather than several weeks. Other benefits of our approach have included making it easier to attract field probation officers, and others, to co-work groups with us without holiday periods and other commitments getting in the way.

## Ownership

It was important that the project was owned from an early stage by both attenders and their probation officers. A crucial first step was the setting up of a steering group to comment on and shape the Unit's work, with representatives from each probation team in Newcastle. Colleagues outside the Unit were also encouraged to come in and co-lead some of the groupwork, though a member of the Unit's staff is always the designated course leader. This gives staff, we hope, a positive, structured groupwork experience without too much involvement in the time consuming, irksome planning stages. We see a definite training role for us here, and this is underlined by our willingness to take students on placement, both as a pure groupwork experience or as part of a fieldwork placement. A format for assessing students' performance is a feature of the Unit's monitoring and evaluation procedures.

## Monitoring, evaluation and refinement

It is, we believe, important that projects have at least some independent, external monitoring. We are fortunate in having two sources for this, though less lucky in that neither (at the time of writing) has yet produced a final report. The Home Office has monitored all Intensive Probation Programmes' data closely. A partnership with Newcastle University in the early days led to a successful bid for funding for a large scale qualitative research project, including interviews with attenders, probation staff and sentencers, as well as statistical analysis. In addition, Unit staff routinely carry out their own monitoring procedures. They produce, with the assistance of Northumbria Probation Service's computer section, a quarterly breakdown of referrals and commencements by probation team and course, analyses of attenders' ages, genders, offending history, ethnicity and so on. This enables us, for example, to target probation teams and individual officers who refer least, or less successfully, to the project. We can also plan the following year's course calendar by assessing the demand for particular modules. As well as looking at quantitative monitoring, each course is evaluated fully by course leaders and a written account produced. This work is invaluable in refining and constantly improving course content. An important feature of this review is the feedback sheets completed on each day of a course by those clients attending. These include attempts to measure attitudinal change over the course of a module. A spin-off from producing detailed write-ups of courses (attenders' names are not included) has been a large number of sales of these to other areas of the country, particularly to probation services interested in setting up their own groupwork projects. As well as these write-ups, each referring probation officer also gets an individual report back on his/her clients, with any areas identified for future work.

## The time factor

The luxury of having time to evaluate and refine our work did not come about by chance and is worthy of mention. Too often groupwork in the probation service is carried out on a goodwill basis by staff who are already busy, even overworked. It is done without proper thought to resource allocation. The Newcastle Unit is a project where resource issues were considered at the outset and an adequate, full time staffing level was set. This was two, later three probation officers, plus a budget for hiring venues, client travel and subsistence, materials, sessional staff and so on. Job descriptions were written, and the programme planned to build in time for planning and evaluation. This avoided the treadmill approach which characterises some probation centres, for example, with a resulting loss of staff morale and motivation. Planning and review time is a great luxury nowadays but is, we believe, crucial to successful groupwork.

## The paperwork

A key principle of our programme is that its operation should be as user friendly as possible for attenders, sentencers and referring probation officers. This is tied in with a belief in good, professionally produced publicity material and a slick, glossy corporate image. This is no substitute, of course, for a quality product, but we believe we offer that too. There are various elements to all this. Referral forms, for example, are single sided, even though they include a wealth of information sufficient for subsequent monitoring, thus eliminating the need for us to trouble staff later for statistics. We believe that many people have a mental block about filling in any form which runs to more than one side of paper (quite right too). Information sheets for sentencers (and institutions, for we take many attenders on a Temporary Release basis) are A4 size and also single sided, therefore ideal for being attached to Pre Sentence Court Reports. The corresponding information sheets for prospective attenders are, on the other hand, pocket sized, use more everyday language and feature good, professional art work. Even the titles of courses are designed to attract rather than repel: 'Keeping your Head' (anger management) and 'Working towards Employment'. Each course also has a professionally designed A3 size poster, again with striking art work in our house style. These are placed in the reception area of each probation office, hostel etc. in the city a few weeks before each course, with a stack of information sheets. We have been surprised at how many clients comment on these posters, take a copy of the information sheets and ask about attendance.

## Partnership

The concept of 'partnership' with other agencies is a topical one for probation services and, at its best, has been seen to be an effective way of working. Part of our philosophy is to introduce clients to community resources they may use after their brief involvement with us. We also believe we do not have a monopoly of skills and that, therefore, other agencies have a lot to offer us in working together. Thus various modules of the programme have been delivered jointly with outside agencies, often using their premises, though our staff remain as overall course leaders, as with any other co-working arrangement. The Employment Course, for example, is run by one probation officer, one careers officer and a member of staff from the Employment Service. Most of the partnerships in which we are involved are finance free (as such work falls within the remit of the organisations involved) though our budget does allow us to buy in expertise if necessary. As well as assisting with the core group work programme, partnerships have also enabled us to broaden what we do on the fringes of this, given that we try to offer attenders various opportunities for constructive activity after their groupwork experience. A good example would be the setting up in 1991 of a motor vehicle project as a follow-on to our 'Car Crime' module. NACRO were brought in as partners, money was raised from outside the probation service and premises (a factory unit) leased from Newcastle Council. We avoided the expense of providing a driving track by leasing some Ministry of Defence land in Northumberland, including an airfield and perimeter road. This proved an unlikely, but cost effective partnership. Northumbria Police were also extremely helpful. On a larger scale, NACRO were encouraged to bid successfully for a two year Home Office funded arts and drama project (Scope), with two full time staff. A significant feature of Scope's work has been a number of fairly ambitious drama productions on offence related themes, such as drugs, domestic violence, and car crime, which have toured local schools and also been presented at probation service conferences. An important spin off from our close working relationship with NACRO has been the cross over into groupwork of some drama techniques (see below).

## Working with men...and women

Paradoxically, though most offenders are young males, we first came to consider the particular implications of working with men through our emphasis on providing substantive equality for women offenders. The disadvantages women suffer in the criminal justice system are well documented and beyond the scope of this chapter. In its work with women, the Unit has attempted to enhance the attractiveness of the Probation Order to sentencers in appropriate cases by offering a range of women-only groups and activities, using female staff. In addition to the structured groupwork, Newcastle Probation Centre is now reserved, exclusively and less formally, to women attenders one day per week. In designing the content of these initiatives we became aware of a variety of issues to be considered. We opted, for example, for a shorter day for the women's courses (10 a.m. till 3 p.m.) to assist those with school age children. The provision of creche facilities, or child minding costs, was another obvious example. The factors in the choice of venue became important too: accessible, non-threatening and 'woman friendly'. Clearly, the content of courses also had to be researched and designed for women's needs, using the best of what was available in the UK and from abroad – more often than not we designed our own. Topics chosen, such as women's offending, stress and assertiveness, were identified in consultation with the women themselves. All this effort paid off and in the second year of operation women constituted almost 25 per cent of our attenders. A development from this was the attention it focused on our work with male offenders.

The choice of venues for courses is, in some ways, as important when working with men as with women. We had to choose places on neutral territory in the city centre and close to bus routes. When running courses in partnership with other agencies we also had to take care to consider how their premises might be seen by offenders. Some apparently felt stigmatised by attending a local NHS drugs facility and the 'drug problems' course was later moved to a neutral venue.

Our approach to groupwork techniques also had to be questioned and refined. Many offenders did not have successful school careers and the traditional 'flip chart and pen' method of groupwork can be reminiscent of the classroom and so off-putting to many. We do use flip charts but tend to prepare them in advance to a high standard on our drawing board wherever possible. Overhead projection slides can be brought in to give some relief to the didactic parts of a programme. Where possible, however, we prefer to use other media to break up a day (remembering that the courses are full time over three to five consecutive days). Techniques include viewing and discussing pre-recorded tapes (we have developed the necessary editing skills to cut out the boring bits), collage work where offenders cut up magazines and create their own composite pictures on a given theme, small group work, the inevitable role play and, increasingly, the use of drama. Rather than draw, for example, a strip cartoon of a particular offence (a common exercise and effective enough) course members may be asked to act it out, positioning other members and freezing the various scenes. If these can be recorded with a Polaroid camera, a story board can be built up. Perhaps the best way to illustrate our work with male offenders in some detail is to describe the process of, and thinking behind, two of the men only courses – 'Keeping your Head' and 'Relationships for Men'.

**Keeping your head**

This, the Unit's anger management course for male offenders, acts as a cornerstone of our approach to groupwork with men. 'Keeping Your Head' (KYH) runs for four consecutive days between 10 a.m. and 4 p.m. Course members and facilitators remain together throughout, including breaks and meal times when informal discussion and social interaction take place. This proximity helps to generate a sense of ownership, which is a common feature of all courses. However, it is particularly important as a means of producing a supportive and enabling atmosphere. On courses such as KYH, where the core subject matter is of such an emotive nature, men attending the course need to become established and comfortable without any unnecessary pressures.

The pre-course information clarifies the aims of the course, which are to explore the causes and consequences of violent and aggressive behaviour; to examine this on an individual basis, but at the same time taking account of cultural and gender based factors which underpin violence. Course attenders are encouraged to focus on coping and assertiveness skills and to develop strategies to absorb trigger points and deal more appropriately with stress.

*Summary of the programme*

**Day One**

The establishment of ground rules is an important feature of every group. KYH is no different and the ground rules include: the prohibition of abusive language and behaviour, alcohol misuse and drug taking. An emphasis on mutual respect and safety is placed high on the agenda, including acceptance of the views and opinions of group members. The average make up of a course such as KYH may include up to six men attending as a condition of temporary release from prison. Specific ground rules relating to these men, as opposed to other participants, need to be established in a clear and straightforward manner. Though men attending on a temporary release basis have volunteered to attend the course, prisons expect attendance to be complete and, clearly, this requires slightly different ground rules compared to offenders from the community.

Following a warm-up round such as a name based exercise, group members are asked to share their expectations of the four days. This can be done using an individual or pairs exercise (depending on the size of the group) feeding back to the group via a flip chart. At this point some notional idea of the group's direction is gauged. Remarks such as, "I want to find out what makes me 'blow'", "...understand why I lose control", "...prevent future loss of temper", are common. Equally, there is often reference to the level of coercion behind a client's attendance, e.g., "My probation officer has asked me to come", "The judge ordered me to deal with my aggression problem" (never conditional in any course), or "I want to get back to my wife and kids". This gives an indication of a client's personal motivation. However, it is important that many of these factors are pushed to one side and that men attending accept that they are participating for their own sake and with some acknowledgement that they have intrinsic difficulties with their aggression towards others.

A follow-up session to this explores the reasons for and against using violence. We brainstorm members' beliefs about aggression and violence, including their views on when they think it is appropriate to hit out and against whom. Many men will often have entrenched views about being aggressive. This is commonly based upon gender roles and rituals which are reinforced by their cultural identity. 'Geordies' are not unique in this respect, yet traditional male values and the part violence plays are always major hurdles for local men to acknowledge. This is true of the Keeping Your Head course but also of other programmes which we run for men.

The first teaching input on the Keeping Your Head course concerns a model for understanding the progression of violence from the initial trigger point. The 'Five Steps' model (Illustration I) suggests a progression of stages involving a loss of control and subsequent depression. A short video recording has been used in the past to introduce this session depicting a scene at a DSS benefits office where a male claimant and his female partner suffer the indignities of being kept waiting only to find out their giro payment will not be forthcoming. The resulting loss of control and aggression which follows is analysed by the group according to the 'Five Steps' model (Illustration I in the chapter Appendix). It has become more common on recent KYH courses to ask the group facilitators to role play this scenario, occasionally with assistance from volunteers in the group. This serves a better purpose in that additional social barriers are broken down and the group process is enhanced in a positive manner.

The day continues with a session exploring triggers and leads to an acknowledgement that what provokes one individual may not necessarily cause the same level of annoyance to another person. Among each group there are always examples given of completely irrational triggers, such as the way someone looks or speaks.

An exercise called '5WH' which is used to analyse actual incidents or offences involving violence concludes the main programme for the day. Attenders are asked to analyse a real incident from their experience in terms of 'who, what, where, when, why and how'. This form of offence analysis, based on the notion of a logical (if misguided) progression towards offending behaviour, has been widely used in the probation service. It was first developed for individual offence related work with offenders by McGuire and Priestley[3]. We find that this type of individualised exercise still has a place within our groupwork programme. Members can be assisted with the actual analysis, but it is during the feedback where opportunity for peer evaluation is most significant: "Why did you do that? …. you could have easily done…".

KYH concludes each day with some form of 'positive strokes'

session and, if the group consents, a time of relaxation or quiet. We also encourage men to use a 'time-out' mechanism during the day whenever necessary, to avoid the build up of tension or frustration. One group facilitator (usually from three on KYH) will accompany a person who, for whatever reason, takes this step. It is helpful to have a quiet room available away from the group for this purpose.

At the close, we find it is essential not only to evaluate the group process of that day, but also to record comments about each individual. These include their level of involvement and factors which appear relevant to their offending or aggression problems. In this way subsequent days can be re-shaped, facilitators can determine particular approaches to assist individuals and, overall, we are in a better position to provide a fuller and more accurate assessment at the end of the course. Clients also complete their own evaluation forms at the end of each day of a course.

**Day Two**

After an optional warm-up and reprise of the previous day's work the main theme of the second day of Keeping Your Head, entitled 'Assertiveness', is introduced. Using typed hand-outs and brief video clips we engage the group in demonstrations of assertiveness, aggression and passivity. Role play is once again used to explore the characteristics of each form of behaviour. Traditional scenarios, such as returning faulty goods to a shop, allow men in the group to act out ways of being more assertive and less aggressive. We ask people to examine the verbal and non-verbal cues which relate to their behaviour. These are amplified with subsequent teaching inputs on 'body language' and interpreting facial expressions using photographs and drawings.

One aspect of this role playing which always produces an impact within the group is the notion of personal space. Men are often less socially intimate than women and we find many examples of the build up of mistrust and aggression that has initially stemmed from an invasion of one's personal space. Machismo is another significant feature and men in the group will admit to giving off signals in public intended to present themselves as 'hard' and 'not to be messed with'. Self-image remains a large determining factor in analysing male violence and we therefore encourage men in our groups to come to terms with this.

Further role plays based on real incidents in attenders' lives conclude the second day. These are video recorded (again with consent) giving participants the option to observe and alter their responses, check out feelings and determine the impact of various verbal and non-verbal signals.

Relaxation and group feedback close the day.

**Day Three**

Two features dominate the third day of Keeping Your Head. These are negotiation and anger control. Following the usual beginning to the day the theme of negotiation is explored. We brainstorm situations in which negotiation normally takes place and try to identify the behavioural factors which support successful negotiation. Situational role plays in pairs are undertaken followed by a brief teaching input suggesting key points to follow. Group members may offer their own scripts for these role plays, but there are also many common examples within an employer/worker relationship or any domestic transaction with a partner where a resolution to a problem is sought.

Anger control has to be considered as a central strategy in any attempt to deal with problems of aggression and violence. Men are asked to identify things which tend to provoke them into becoming angry and to offer any associated avoidance strategy they have successfully used. Group discussion reinforces and widens the options which are available in given situations. A list of 'ways of controlling my temper' is drawn up at this stage as a reminder for the future.

Additional exercises about provocation take this one step further and attempt to develop an awareness of the inner self, based on an examination of thoughts, feelings and actions when provoked. This utilises Gestalt theory which emphasises the inter-relatedness of these and other factors within the whole personal experience.

One method we use breaks 'provocation' down into four stages. These are:–

(i)    preparing for provocation

(ii)   confronting the provocation

(iii)  coping with arousal and agitation, and

(iv)  self-reward.

Arising from this, group members begin to see anger management as more of a process which they can, at times, heavily influence. For men who are traditionally not expected to be in tune with their inner self, who feel, but seldom attempt to form any explanation for these feelings, this can be an emancipating experience and one which is rewarding, in the same way as finding a new labour saving tool.

The overriding aim at this stage of the course is to encourage men to make sense of their experience of provocation and begin to learn to talk themselves down in difficult situations. This is, in essence, the flip-side of the 'Five Steps' model.

**Day Four**

An interesting warm-up that we always tend to reserve for the last day of the course is a round on 'One good thing about last night'. It's simple enough and produces a quick round of positives to start the day. We state at the outset that nothing to do with violence, intimidation, or discrimination is acceptable. Once again, it is important that men in the group are praised and encouraged to feel good about themselves in pursuit of essentially non-traditional male responses.

Following on from the development of anger control strategies on Day Three, the morning is spent formulating responses to criticism. A teaching input with the use of video demonstrates appropriate and inappropriate responses to criticism. Pairs exercises support this and role play is optional depending upon time available and interest.

A summary of the central concepts of the course follows this in preparation for the final afternoon of the four days which draws together objectives, personal action plans and highlights the process of change as a sequential model, i.e. based on significant inter-related steps.

'Keeping Your Head' takes on men who have shown an inability to control their aggression often resulting in extreme forms of violence. The programme offers participants, within four days, the opportunity to begin to understand their behaviour and develop strategies for change. KYH may be the first step on a self-directed process of rediscovery, or it may form part of a broader package of supervision involving other courses. Each person who attends the programme receives a detailed written report together with all exercise material and supporting hand-outs from the course. Personal evaluations include suggestions for future work, which field probation officers may integrate in to their individual supervision plans.

Whilst the course covers mainstream areas of anger control, a notable omission is any detailed attempt to explain masculinity, or inter-generational violence. Victim awareness is one other area we deal with superficially at present. However, these are issues which we find frequently permeate group discussion and also vary greatly between individuals and from course to course.

One major issue which has arisen from the experience of running KYH is that we have found men who attend this course are often able to acknowledge substantial levels of violence attributed to themselves, particularly when this involves confrontations with other men. However, these same individuals are frequently dismissive about their violence towards more vulnerable groups such as women and children. They tend to be extremely guarded about their level of confrontation with partners and the abuse of power within personal relationships which underpins domestic violence.

In the last 12 months the Intensive Probation Unit has developed a complementary programme to Keeping Your Head intended to address this subject. We set about designing a course, again exclusively for men, who were abusive to their female partners. 'Relationships for Men', the resulting course, aims to assist men who have current relationship difficulties and who acknowledge that their behaviour is a factor in this. Their behaviour may not necessarily have involved the use of direct physical violence to a partner, or have resulted in recorded convictions.

Planning for the course involved liaison with other organisations and groups in various parts of the country who were involved in working with men who perpetrate domestic violence. Attendance at two national network practitioners' meetings,[4] and a subscription to 'Working with Men' magazine,[5] were particularly helpful. We found, however, little agreement nationally on the best policy and strategy for working with perpetrators of domestic violence. Nevertheless, as a result of support and advice received, and collaboration with colleagues in Northumbria Probation Service, a course programme was developed and successfully piloted in June 1994. The following is a brief summary of the actual course.

**Relationships for Men**

Six referrals were received for the course. These included four men currently serving prison sentences, two of whom were refused temporary release. One person from the community withdrew prior to the course and a second failed to attend. The course therefore commenced with two men, both on temporary release licence from prison. They completed the three day programme in full.

The group was facilitated by two men. This was largely for pragmatic reasons. As a Unit, we were influenced by the apparent trend among more established groups towards a mixed gender leadership. This remains contentious but has been agreed in principle by our staff group.

*Content*

At the planning stage, six core areas were identified, each of one half day. They were: relationships, power and control, inter-generational violence, masculinity, effective communication and equality. The programme was developed for a group of 8–10 men using a variety of techniques including role play and pairs work. This was slightly amended in the knowledge of an expected low attendance.

**Day One**

Following a short introduction to the course and members' names, we began with reference to a list of key principles (Illustration II in the chapter Appendix). Together with a broad definition of domestic violence, the subject was introduced and general expectations shared. Another feature of the programme was an 'issues/sexist terms' sheet, attached to the wall. We decided, on the basis of inherent sexism in the debate, to defer dealing with sexist language issues to the end of each session but to log examples, without comment, as they occurred. We began the day's programme proper with a discussion about the roles that men and women take in relationships and identified some of the stereotypes in our society. This led to a debate about the power differential invested in these roles and subsequent control patterns which evolve to maintain and support this system. Dysfunction was examined in terms of a breakdown of communication between partners, failure to express emotions, poor anger control and features of masculinity. The morning was concluded with a sequence from a video entitled 'Do Men Hate Women?', which further identified the power and control facet of domestic/relationship disharmony.

The second part of the day continued the theme of power and control. We examined individual danger signals indicating a loss of control, including physical and emotional signals and ritualistic imagery. An exercise called 'The Male Emotional Funnel System' (Illustration III in the Appendix) explained the way in which the range of emotions men experience are often funnelled into anger and rage by traditional masculine constraints. The 'Power & Control Wheel' (Illustration IV in the Appendix) was used to broaden understanding of quite subtle and sophisticated methods of controlling women within relationships. This led to discussion about the cost of partner abuse from the victim's perspective. At the close, both men were asked to complete a piece of homework. This was a questionnaire on masculine expectations of power and control. They were asked to involve their partner in this exercise, if willing.

**Day Two**

After a recap on the previous day, the morning of Day Two focused upon inter-generational violence. We began with a Channel Four video, 'Pulling the Punches', which gave details of a case history and also demonstrated some of the work of the Everyman Centre in Brixton. Both participants later described their own experience of suffering male violence, as children.

A teaching input followed which offered a model to understand violent incidents[6]. This focused upon the personal appraisal system of triggers, e.g. 'you're doing that deliberately', which is a common factor that can lead to anger and aggression. The model also highlighted irritants, costs and transgressions within relationships.

The second part of the day opened up a debate on masculinity.

Exercises were used to evoke responses about 'Real Men' and heroes or models. Important messages such as 'men often put on brave faces' and 'men are scared about being labelled soft', helped towards recognition of the societal and cultural environment which supports the suppression of male emotions. Myths of male sexuality opened another theme, where men's sexual expression can underpin other forms of control and abuse.

**Day Three**

The final day set out to make links between abusive behaviour in relationships and methods of promoting equality and mutual respect. The morning adopted assertiveness training to develop the concepts of effective communication and positive self-talk. Throughout each session we also made reference to the more familiar counter scenario where introspection and denial predominate and where resentment and loss of control lead to violence.

The afternoon of Day Three continued the theme of equality. Strategies to avoid the escalation of conflict such as 'time outs' were discussed. Another important topic was negotiation. In these exercises each person provided 'rules of thumb' to promote understanding and compromise. The final exercise was 'Steps to Change', showing change as a process of manageable steps including an acknowledgement of particular strengths and weaknesses.

*Process*

Both men who undertook the course interacted well and within a short period of time had developed a consistent level of trust. This certainly enhanced the development of the course which otherwise could have taken a different and less appealing inward turn. Each day the men took exercise material home and subsequently asked for further copies of the packs. They said that they had shared this work with their partners and wanted to build up further systems of support to continue the process.

*Summary*

Despite the low numbers, the experience proved successful. Two male facilitators allowed for, at times, very easy interaction with the men, but on other occasions a female worker could have enhanced the process without being singled out or viewed differently. The level of sexism was not high, it appeared, and very little was discussed separately from the programme. It is acknowledged, however, that male collusion, conscious or unconscious, was higher than would have been normal in a mixed gender facilitated group.

## Conclusion

This has been the story of one approach to working with men and no doubt there are many different ways of achieving the same ends. In all cases, however, we believe that structural aspects of project design are at least as important as programme content. Ours is not, it must be acknowledged, the cheapest of designs. The high ratio of course leaders to participants, the use of community based venues, our insistence on high quality materials, and the time built in to the project to allow evaluation and development are just some of the factors which increase unit costs at a time when it often seems that 'cheapest' is seen as 'best'. We make little apology for this, but it makes projects very vulnerable in a period of cost cutting, especially as voluntary groupwork programmes are not a statutory requirement of probation services, merely an added bonus.

We have learned a lot from our experiences and have been particularly pleased and surprised at the generally positive and even enthusiastic feedback, including indications of significant attitude change, from our attenders. Some have been hard work, but it is often these who make the most positive comments. Many attenders have voted with their feet and come back several times to attend different modules within the programme. The seeking of consumer views is still relatively rare in probation practice, but it is to be encouraged rather than feared.

If we had more time there is probably much more that could be done in terms of liaison with magistrates, judges and lawyers, selling the concept of the Unit as a whole and, particularly, the principle of voluntary attendance. The occasional meeting and the periodic circulation of publicity material and our annual reports are generally the best which can be achieved. Similarly, more contact with probation staff might be desirable; despite our efforts some still refer offenders to us far more than others. Keeping customers satisfied is never easy, especially after the novelty of a new initiative wears off, though we have more than maintained the high attendance levels set in year one of the project.

Part of the brief for writing this chapter was to consider how we might, with hindsight, have done it all differently. In general we wouldn't. It may, however, have been sensible to split the male and female modules from the outset rather than vainly trying to achieve a mixed programme. This attempt lasted a few months and only served to disadvantage the lower numbers of female offenders and to dilute the impact of our material through the search for an elusive lowest common denominator. This realisation was the trigger we needed to begin a thorough analysis of what working with men is all about.

### References and notes

1.    Mair, G. et al. (1994) 'Intensive Probation in England and Wales: An Evaluation' HORS 136, London: HMSO.

2.    Ross, R. R. (1991) 'Reasoning and Rehabilitation of Offenders' *Conference Proceedings: What Works? Effective Methods to Reduce Re-offending*, April 1991, Greater Manchester Probation Service.

3.    McGuire, J. and Priestley, P. (1985) *Offending Behaviour – Skills and Stratagems for Going Straight,* London: Batsford Academic.

4.    The national network is an association of individuals and agencies involved in domestic violence work. At present there is no formal structure nor secretariat. The network holds meetings twice each year and conferences for practitioners. Details are available from any member, such as Nottingham AGENDA, 202 Mansfield Road, Nottingham. NG1 3HX.

5.    *Working with Men* magazine, T. Lloyd and T. Wood (eds.) 320 Commercial Way, London. SE15 1QN.

6.    Frude, N. (1994) *Helping Violent People to Change.* The Association for Psychological Therapies (On-site Course) Northumbria Probation Service. February 1994.

**APPENDIX**

*Illustration I*

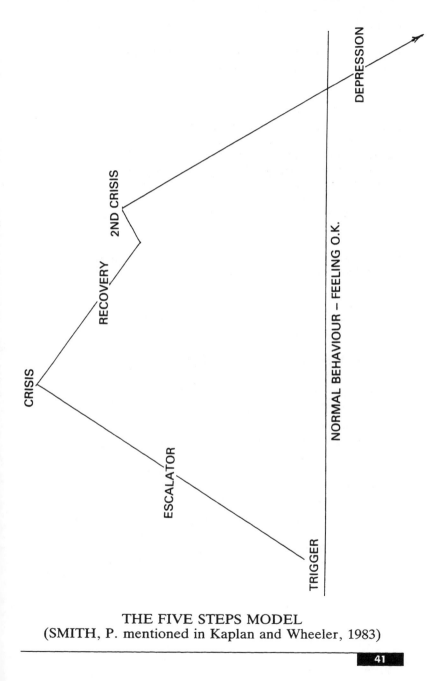

THE FIVE STEPS MODEL
(SMITH, P. mentioned in Kaplan and Wheeler, 1983)

### *Illustration II*

## INTENSIVE PROBATION UNIT

## RELATIONSHIPS FOR MEN COURSE.

### KEY PRINCIPLES

1    Abuse is a learned behaviour.

2.    People can change.

3.    Perpetrators are responsible for their violence.

4.    Assault is a criminal offence and should be treated accordingly.

5.    Violence is not caused by drugs or stress.

6.    Any kind of violence is unacceptable.

7.    The safety of women is of paramount importance.

*Illustration III*

# THE MALE EMOTIONAL FUNNEL SYSTEM

Fear
Alarm
Annoyance
Dejection
Depression
Disappointment
Displeasure
Frustration
Guilt
Helplessness
Hurt
Insecurity
Jealousy
Let Down            Transition            Anger ...... Rage ...... Violence
Loneliness
Nervousness
Resentful
Sadness
Troubled
Uncomfortable
Unhappiness
Etc.
Etc.

.

.

.

Anger

*traditional masculine limits*

repeated incidence of
misidentified feelings
push men towards
violence

From: NOTTINGHAM AGENDA: 202 Mansfield Road,
Nottingham. NG1 3HX

## *Illustration IV*

# THE POWER AND CONTROL WHEEL

from
Domestic Abuse Intervention Project
206 West Fourth Street
Duluth, Minnesota

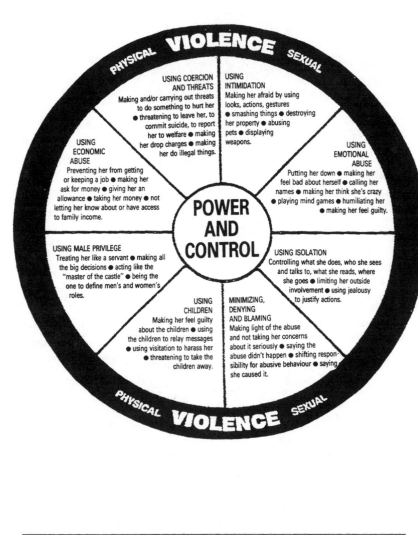

## NORTHUMBRIA PROBATION SERVICE
## NEWCASTLE DIVISION
## INTENSIVE PROBATION UNIT

# KEEPING YOUR HEAD

### FOR INDIVIDUALS WHO WANT TO LEARN MORE EFFECTIVE ANGER CONTROL

A FOUR DAY COURSE
FOR MEN ONLY
FROM 9.45 a.m. – 4.00 p.m.

AT NEWCASTLE PROBATION CENTRE
70-80 BLENHEIM STREET
NEWCASTLE UPON TYNE

### AIM

This course aims to explore the causes and consequences of violent and aggressive behaviour. The central theme of this course is that aggressive incidents tend to follow a predictable pattern consisting of five stages. Participants are asked to look at their own offending, consider how they felt at the time and suggest ways in which they could have dealt with the situation differently. By introducing assertiveness, negotiating skills, and relaxation techniques, the course aims to equip the participants so that they can deal with potentially violent situations without resorting to the use of aggressive behaviour.

### SOME COMMENTS FROM COURSE ATTENDERS

"I have already dealt with situations this week differently."

"I've learnt another option besides violence."

"Been shown other options instead of steaming in."

### PROGRAMME

**Day 1** – provides an introduction to anger/violence and its effects.

**Day 2** – concentrates on encouraging the development of assertiveness skills.

**Day 3** – focuses on enabling individuals to develop alternative coping mechanisms.

**Day 4** – reinforces the mechanisms learnt on Day 3.

This course is part of a modular programme of groupwork and constructive activities offered by:–

NEWCASTLE INTENSIVE
PROBATION UNIT
717 WEST ROAD
NEWCASTLE UPON TYNE
NE15 7PS

TELEPHONE (0191) 2741153

FAX (0191) 2750963

# RELATIONSHIPS

## *A 3 DAY COURSE FOR MEN*

## *CRECHE OR CHILDMINDING AVAILABLE ON REQUEST*

**FOR MORE INFORMATION SEE YOUR PROBATION OFFICER**

# KEEPING YOUR
# HEAD

A 4-DAY COURSE FOR MEN

*Creche Available*

**FOR MORE INFORMATION SEE YOUR PROBATION OFFICER**

# CHAPTER 4

# DRIVING US CRAZY: MOTOR PROJECTS AND MASCULINITY

## Karen Buckley and Karen Young

### Introduction

In this chapter we look at the attraction that cars have for men.
Using the experience of a car crime project in Liverpool, we
consider how work targeted at male car offenders can be
undertaken, the strengths of such work, its possibilities, and its
pitfalls and potential weaknesses. There can be little dispute
about the impact of motor-related crime in the UK. Indeed, it
has been one of the fastest growing phenomena of the last 20
years. Thefts of and from cars have led to rocketing insurance
premiums. The advent of more sophisticated technology and
increased surveillance of driving habits has resulted in rising
convictions for driving under the influence of alcohol. New
kinds of offending have emerged which are discussed endlessly
in the media and even given catchy titles such as 'joyriding',
the contested phrase used to describe the practice of stealing
cars to drive for speed, daring and thrills, often by children
under the age of 14. 'Ramraiding' refers to the use of stolen
cars to break into stores and factories. More recently, the term
'rage driving' has been used to address incidents of violent and
sometimes fatal confrontations between competing drivers
who are otherwise legitimate road users.

The 1992 British Crime Survey (BCS) indicates that one in five
car owners were the victims of car crime in 1991, and that more
than one third of crimes overall involved cars (Mayhew and
Maung, 1992). The risk of car theft is higher in England and
Wales than in any other European country. In 1992, for
example, the police recorded 93 per cent more car-related

crime than in 1982. Looking at car crime over the decade 1981-91, the BCS found an 81 per cent increase in the theft of cars and an 86 per cent increase in theft from cars during that period.

Motor-related offending is thus, in anyone's terms, a major problem. Though patterns of motor crime change over time, the human and financial costs of responding to it never diminish. One of the key questions for us, therefore, is why the motor car has become such a focus for anti-social behaviour. Part of the answer may lie in our very complex attitudes towards driving and cars.

Who are motor offenders and what links them with, or separates them from, the 'average' motorist? One key, and yet often overlooked characteristic, is their maleness. A research project in Northumbria in 1992 found that of 31,000 offenders arrested for vehicle-related offences in 1991, 98.4 per cent were male. The other key characteristic is, perhaps, youth. Work by Briggs in Durham found that 50 per cent of vehicle offences were committed by youths aged between 10 and 17. What these young males share is a macho belief in their own driving prowess (Briggs 1992; Nee and Light, 1992); clearly an exaggerated belief in the light of the accident statistics. Northumbria Police, for example, found offenders who were convinced they could drive better than the police. Surprisingly, however, the gender of offenders is often not remarked upon by researchers, merely taken for granted. Light et al. (1992), for example, comment on their research population: "Most were from the lower socio-economic groups, those who often find themselves on the receiving end of the criminal justice system. This study is therefore uninformative on car offending within other social groups". In looking at driving behaviour, however, it is clear that its gendered character is, in many ways, widely recognised and accepted. It is well known that men are often attracted to fast driving and many not only drive too fast but hold quite unrealistic beliefs about their driving abilities, and for a few especially, even when intoxicated. Furthermore, for many men their status – indeed their masculinity, the way in which they *do* being male – is related to the type of car that they drive and, of course, the way in which they drive it. For many men there is something highly sexual about motoring. And yet, not only do researchers tend to overlook the importance of the question of gender, but for too long, so have practitioners.

One of the difficulties with the way we currently view crime is our tendency to compartmentalise and see offenders as reflecting only one aspect of their behaviour, despite, for example, the research from Corbett and Simon (1992) which shows that serious motoring offenders were generalists. Offenders tend to be viewed as 'burglars' or 'car thieves' or 'violent men', when they may be all these things as well as bad or good partners or employees or citizens. This viewpoint has had an impact on how we respond to offenders. In the past we have tended to construct programmes into which individuals have to fit. Part of our motivation for this is a need to make things manageable from our professional perspective, but it can also feed into an offender's need to belong and to have status. One of the values, thus, of a masculinity-based analysis is that it cuts across most of these boundaries and provides a new point of connection (Buckley, 1995). Masculinity gives clues as to the origins of much anti-social behaviour, whether subject to criminal sanction or not.

Currently, we have two major ways of working with motoring offenders. Probation officers have perhaps tended to individualise the offender, working with his personal problem configuration, of which driving behaviour may be a part. Alternatively, there has been a growth of local projects aimed at engaging with groups of offenders through their pleasure in cars in the hope of diverting them towards legitimate means of fulfilling their quest for excitement. It is this approach that has given rise to what are commonly referred to as 'motor projects'. Motor projects have had their enthusiasts and their detractors. On the positive side, Moore and Lloyd (1992) comment: "The case for motor projects, it seems to us, is not that they have a direct impact on crime, particularly car crime, or even a direct relevance to all those who are convicted of it. It is rather that for some young people who are in trouble or who are vulnerable and troubled, they can provide activities that can retain their interest and offer opportunities and relationships which can increase their self-esteem. Both of these may indirectly have an impact on that involvement in crime."

On the other hand, many probation officers and social workers have worried about exposing offenders who are apparently hooked on speed and thrills to more speed and thrills. Communities and magistrates have been concerned that projects may appear to reward bad behaviour, and fail to include the necessary elements of punishment or rehabilitation. The response in some schemes – the Sutton Wheels project in Nottingham for example – has been to experiment with activities other than car-based ones, such as barge trips, conservation work and the use of bicycles. Motor projects have started to use a variety of methods to attempt to tackle stereotypical masculine behaviours. Increasingly, groups are working on exercises designed to look at masculinity and the pressures facing men. We can get a better indication of some of the issues involved, and some of the methods used in such work, by looking in a certain amount of detail at the operation of one such motor project: the Merseyside Car Offenders Project (COP).

## The Merseyside Car Offenders Project

The impetus for this project derived from the Liverpool Responsible Drivers' Group which was established at one of the city's probation offices in 1989. A pilot programme was set up in 1990 taking referrals from the Liverpool Petty Sessional area. It was originally devised in response to the high rate of vehicle-related crime in the Liverpool area. It reflected the concern of both the public and the courts to the dangerous and anti-social nature of such offences. The target group was offenders who, through repeatedly committing car-related offences, were at risk of custody. Faced with these offenders, courts had few alternatives to imprisonment other than heavy fines or community service. Certainly no disposal was then available which might address such behaviour; the traditional probation order not being considered appropriate by sentencers.

The pilot programme, therefore, found a niche in the offence-focused form of supervision. Participation in the course, as part of a probation order, was designed to offer offenders an opportunity to challenge and confront their attitudes to their repeated involvement in serious driving offences. The focus was on irresponsible attitudes to driving and, consequently, a wide range of vehicle-related offences fell within the ambit of the project. This was considered to be of particular importance with offenders convicted of driving with excess alcohol, in that they were unable to distance themselves from the criminal nature of their actions. It was not assumed that such an offence should be equated with alcohol dependency, but rather, gross irresponsibility. Whenever dependency did appear to have dictated the offender's behaviour, however, the referral was rejected as falling outside the programme's focus.

In March 1992 Merseyside Probation Service established a working party to examine the nature and extent of car-related crime in the region and to determine the most appropriate response. During the period in which the working party was meeting, the probation service made a successful funding application to the Urban Crime Fund to establish a responsible driving and vehicle maintenance project in partnership with the voluntary sector. The combined potential of a multi-agency, offence-focused groupwork programme informed by practice experience and research nationally, together with the driving and vehicle maintenance elements, provided the framework within which the Car Offenders Project (COP) developed.

**Programme structure and content**

The programme comprises 18 two-hour sessions which are spread over a four-week period. There are two principal elements to the programme. The first is an intensive offence-focused groupwork programme with 12 constituent sessions attended within the first week. Seven of the sessions are led by probation officers and the remaining five are delivered by the COP's partner agencies: Merseyside Police, the Royal Liverpool University Hospital, the Road Safety Service, the Association of British Insurers, and Merseyside Women's Group. Each of the discrete sessions has a particular focus and aims to engage the group participants in exercises which concentrate on the dangers, responsibilities and realities associated with driving. Offending behaviour is explicitly examined and constructively challenged. Individuals are required to reflect upon the consequences of their offences for themselves, their families, their victims (both actual and potential) and for the wider community and society in general.

The second element comprises six two-hour sessions which run over three weeks on a two-session per week basis. They focus on developing the knowledge and skills that are necessary in order to maintain a vehicle in a safe and roadworthy condition. This element concentrates on legal requirements for the purposes of Ministry of Transport certification and related aspects of vehicle maintenance as provided by road traffic legislation.

## Aims and objectives

The principal aim of the COP is to provide the courts with an effective community-based disposal – it is available as a 1a(2) condition in a Probation Order – specifically for the purposes of sentencing offenders who have been convicted of serious car-related crimes. The COP provides tightly structured, disciplined and challenging opportunities for serious offenders to:

(i)   examine the reasons for their offending behaviour;

(ii)  consider the effect which their behaviour has on themselves, their families, their victims and the wider community;

(iii) encourage participants to examine ways of changing their offending behaviour;

(iv)  promote greater understanding of the means to avoid further offences of this nature, via educational inputs from other relevant agencies;

(v)   develop their decision-making and problem solving skills, in order that they may develop strategies for avoiding further offending, bearing in mind the constraints of disqualification.

## Target group

The COP has as its 'target group' all offenders aged 17 years plus who have been convicted of motor vehicle offences for which a custodial sentence can be imposed, for example, reckless/dangerous driving or driving whilst disqualified, and for whom such a sentencing option is a distinct possibility. The programme does not engage offenders who have been convicted of alcohol-related offences, as Merseyside Probation Service offers an alternative specialist Alcohol Impaired Drivers' Programme for such offenders. Referrals are made at the pre-sentence report (PSR) preparation stage and are considered by COP core staff. Assessments are informed by the COP aims and objectives and the legal framework, which is the legislation and national standards governing probation orders. Tight gatekeeping means that COP is only offered to the courts as a PSR proposal in cases which are compatible with the project's target group.

To reiterate, to be eligible for inclusion on the COP,

participants have to be facing the serious risk of custody for their offending. Social services clients from 16 years of age are also accepted following a thorough assessment interview to consider their level of maturity and their commitment to challenging their offending behaviour in a group setting. In addition, social services clients have to have been through the full range of social service community-based disposals such as Intermediate Treatment programmes. Those clients are placed on a Supervision Order.

Martin and Webster (1994) suggest that clients referred to motor projects in England and Wales can roughly be placed into two main groups. The first type is the younger offender who is involved in 'Taking without the owner's consent' (TWOC) whom, they suggest, have moved onto other offences once they have passed 17. However, in our experience, clients charged with TWOC or aggravated motor vehicle theft (AUTMV) can be found in all age groups. One recent referral to the project was a 46 year-old man charged with AUTMV. The second type of client they describe has usually been charged with driving whilst disqualified and without insurance as driving bans have been imposed for earlier motor vehicle-related offending. These tend to be older offenders and Martin and Webster's observation that, "The older group may have grown through the stage of incessant twocking...and be looking for a way to get legal and settle down", coincides with our experience of clients of the Car Offenders Programme. Moreover, however, in our opinion the two groups are bound together both by their continued obsession with the motor car and its associations with masculinity.

COP's focus on masculinity has meant that few problems have been experienced in running mixed age range groups, for there is a commonality of experience in respect of their relationship to motor vehicles. Older participants can readily identify with notions of masculinity expressed by 'joyriding' participants, whilst also being useful group members in spontaneously and actively challenging more outrageous expressions of bravado from younger members of the group. Older participants can admit to involving themselves in potentially life-threatening situations on the roads, such as speeding and competitive and aggressive driving. A small proportion will also admit to high speed chases involving the police when they have been attempting to avoid arrest. Like younger participants, many will view themselves as having a 'right' to drive, and fail to see the potential dangers and consequences of driving with no insurance or licence.

The COP's client group has been, and continues to be, predominantly male. To date, the programme has had only six women referred by field probation officers. One of these women received a custodial sentence, and five received probation orders with the 1a(2) condition. Three women successfully completed the programme, and two women had the condition deleted on medical grounds. The women who completed the programme were all given the opportunity to bring a female friend, or the chance to delay their starting date to allow the opportunity of being with other female participants. None of the three women took up these offers. To ensure the needs of these women were met, all groups had female groupworkers.

**Oppressive language**

Challenging oppressive language and behaviour has always been integral to COP and is a vital element in terms of challenging masculinity. Clients are assisted in the process of recognising how their day-to-day interactions can negatively impact not only on themselves, but also on those around them. Prior to acceptance on the programme clients are required to sign a contract which, amongst other codes of behaviour, states, "I agree to show respect to all persons, and will not be racist, sexist or any way offensive towards others". Clients are thus made aware from first contact that neither oppressive language nor oppressive behaviour will be tolerated. Clients not agreeing to this have been deemed unsuitable for the programme.

Project rules are reinforced on the first session, and throughout the programme. Participants are made aware of how, why and when oppressive language will be challenged, and why breach action will be enforced if this is persistent. Participants will often test boundaries of how far unacceptable language or behaviour will be tolerated. Presenting a united front with other group leaders when tackling this cannot be stressed too strongly. It is, therefore, important for groupworkers to discuss and reach a consensus as to what constitutes anti-oppressive practice and to determine by whom, and how, this will be enforced and incorporated in the programme. Co-leading with female groupworkers often poses far fewer problems in this area. However, male group leaders who do provide support can act as powerful role models in an all male group by pushing the boundaries of stereotypical male interactions. When challenging sexist language, for example, male group leaders will take this beyond the realm of being a women's 'problem'. By the same token, racist language, when challenged by white workers can have much more power within the group.

The benefits of consistently challenging language can be seen when participants openly correct themselves when using oppressive language or, at best, adopt different ways of communicating within the group. This process also provides a safe environment for men, when encouraging the expression of feelings and emotions. This is important, for instance, when participants are taken to the Royal Liverpool Hospital during the programme. Here they are shown quite disturbing material portraying the consequences of car accidents. Many participants will subsequently relive, and relate, experiences they have personally been involved in, or in which they have seen friends die in car crashes. Many may never have allowed themselves to freely express feelings such as being frightened, remorseful or guilty as a result of such situations. Engaging in this process allows participants to begin to empathise with potential victims of their continuing behaviour.

For men to enter such discussions can be a difficult and painful experience. It is, therefore, important for group participants to be aware that any attempts to sabotage personal disclosures, such as dismissing, or talking over other participants, or making inappropriate comments about their sexuality (for example, the expression of feelings and emotions often seen as 'feminine' and thus equated with homosexuality) will not be tolerated, but challenged. To assist this process anti-oppressive guidelines have been drawn up for group leaders on the COP.

**The programme**

Day One begins with an ice breaker session called the 'Brief Driving History'. Participants are asked to fill in a very short questionnaire regarding their experiences with cars and their offending background. We have found that this session is vital for establishing the framework of challenging masculinity which continues throughout the week. Perhaps the most important questions from this exercise are:

How old were you when you first drove?

What type of vehicle was it?

Who owned the car?

What would be your ideal car and why?

Most participants will readily admit to driving cars from 14-15 years of age, some being as young as 11, using bricks on the pedals, or cushions to enable them to see over the steering wheel. For participants initiated into 'joyriding' it is typical that the cars used were those dumped on working class housing estates by older boys. Many participants view their behaviour to have been 'normal', and based on a fundamental belief that, "It's a boy's thing," and an aspect of a boy's rite of passage into manhood prior to establishing a permanent settled relationship.

Participants often claim to have become 'addicted' to the adrenalin rush that 'joyriding' can bring, viewing their behaviour as uncontrollable. Very often, however, participants appear to have absorbed the media presentation of this phenomenon and use it as a means of abdicating responsibility for their behaviour. If one agrees with the statement, "It is an addiction", which may be the case for a small number of 'joyriders', logically one must find a 'fix' or 'cure'. In our view this had led to the establishment of projects which focus on competitive motor racing as the 'cure' to this illness.

By looking beyond such a simplistic explanation and delving into the pressures participants have faced and felt in relation to the use of, or theft of, cars, a wider picture emerges. Participants admit that there is a strong pressure to engage in such activities in order to maintain friendships. It is viewed as critical to gaining status and prestige amongst their peer group. In particular, admiration is gained by stealing high performance cars, driving and testing them to their limit, and being able to control such vehicles in life-threatening circumstances. Such behaviour is equated with being a 'real man' and feelings attached to this can, in some cases, be powerful. One participant described feeling, "Like Jesus" in such situations.

Answers provided by participants give a lot of scope for

delving further into male and female socialisation and, in particular, into why participants feel that few girls, if any, are involved in 'joyriding'. When exploring boys' initiation into car use it is also the case that older family members, such as brothers, fathers, uncles, may have shown them how to drive. This often leads in to discussions of whether participants feel family members have provided inappropriate role models in respect of male behaviour, and whether this impacted on their subsequent offending behaviour. Some will admit that this can lead to the assumption that driving is OK, as, "Everyone does it". One recent participant admitted that his father had always been an illegal driver and thus when he himself drove illegally he did not see it either as criminal or as dangerous. Finally, in examining another question asked of all participants – what would be your ideal car? – and asking each participant to give one reason why they have chosen that particular model of car, the groundwork is prepared for the next day's session on 'the image of the car'. The reasons typically given for choosing particular models are, "Speed", "Makes me more attractive to women", and other things to do with image and power.

**Toys for the boys: Go-karting**

Go-karting was initially placed on the programme in response to the perceived need to divert car offenders into legal alternatives to finding a 'buzz' or excitement from driving. It was also placed on the timetable in direct contrast with the hospital session that followed. The hospital session uses accident slides of victims or drivers of cars involved in accidents. This illustrates the potential dangers of 'joyriding', driving at high speeds, under the influence of drink and/or drugs and, when young men, often together, are attempting to find a buzz or excitement from driving.

Go-karting tracks have been established to recreate the feel of motor car rally racing, with timed laps and an overall winner subsequently established. To avoid the worst excesses of this, laps were not timed, participants' starting times were staggered and participants were advised that any competitive racing would lead to them being taken off the track. Too often the intentions of the work were undermined by the attraction of competition. Indeed, as David Jackson (1992) has argued, "Go-kart racing schemes or police invitations to young men to handle fast performance cars in controlled situations are like inviting alcoholics to a brewery".

Participants would often boast of winning certain laps. A pecking order could quickly be established in respect of the best driver in terms of speed or ability to manoeuvre the go-kart on tight bends. It was also interesting, although unsurprising, to see male groupworkers become as competitive on the tracks as male participants. It could be daunting for female workers to use go-karts, and indeed one female participant, aged 46, refused to participate in this session. Female groupworkers did not compete on the track and tended to drive slower than their male colleagues. This could lead to derision from male participants calling them 'Sunday drivers', and could reinforce participants' views of women as 'bad' drivers, when good driving skills are, for them, associated with taking risks, driving at high speeds, and so on, despite discussions to the contrary.

The view that go-karts can provide a learning experience by distracting participants' energies away from cars seemed questionable. It is clear that go-karting does, to some extent, validate the idea that men should be preoccupied with the speed and excitement of motorised vehicles. One might also question whether participants should spend essential money from either state benefits, or the household budget, in providing a very short 'buzz' (go-karting costs £10 for half an hour). Its appropriateness also needs to be questioned. As an able-bodied sport, the go-karts themselves are often unsuited to people with certain disabilities, those with a 'fuller figure' and people, usually women, under five feet five inches tall. In the event, and on balance, it was decided to replace this sesson, particularly as the overall messages given to participants appeared to be confusing and inappropriate.

**The image of the car**

'The image of the car' session replaced 'Toys for the boys' and was originally based on an exploration of car advertising. It has subsequently been further developed by a lecturer from Liverpool University with extensive experience of teaching media studies. The main aim of the session is to change the way participants look at the car in relation to themselves. The objectives of the session have been to deconstruct the image of the car, and to make participants aware of, and to question, advertising which places the car in the realm of freedom, power and control, sexual desirability, status and fantasy.

Participants for this session are initially split into two groups, and are asked to write their responses on a flipchart to the questions: 'Why do I like cars?' and 'How do I feel when around cars?' A few of the flipcharted answers from recent groups are reproduced below. These give an indication of common themes that evolve and can be focused upon. Answers often reflect discussions and debate from the previous day, and it is often important to expand to these.

### Group A

*Why do I like cars/How do I feel when around them?* (combined answers)

Looks – style – getting attention – flashy – speed – respect – prestige – transport – image – lifestyle – safety – independence – go anywhere you want – freedom – luxury – accessories/CDs/leather seats.

### Group B

*Why do I like cars/How do I feel when around them?* (combined answers)

Image – different cars portray image of driver – fast – speed – go anywhere you want – being in control gives a buzz – adrenalin rush – manoeuvre the car – sharp bends – get to destinations further afield – nice cars attract women – comfort in more powerful, expensive cars.

Groups are then handed cards with a variety of pictures of cars on them. They are asked to say whether they are happy with the car they have been given and who would be the typical driver of such a vehicle. Pictures of high performance cars as well as those of the Robin Reliant and Skoda are deliberately placed within the group as their respective images, without fail, provoke intense reaction and debate from participants. They will invariably want to change their card for one which has a more powerful model. This provides a good focus for discussion and begins to challenge participants' views that cars serve little other purpose than getting from one destination to another. This can be particularly useful when there are disqualified drivers on the course, who claim their car use is only linked to personal convenience and lack of a good public transport system. It is also a useful exercise in exploring why high performance cars are targeted by those who steal. Some of the flipcharted answers from one of the groups are reproduced below.

*VW Beetle*
Happy with car
Reliable
Typical driver: student/trendy/collector's car

*Vauxhall Calibra*
Happy with car
Nice style
Typical driver: executive and/or business person
More individual person's car — male/female with money

*Robin Reliant*
Unhappy with car
Not my style – No power – No style – Unsafe
Typical driver: Old man

*Audi Coupé*
Happy with car
Nice look – comfortable – fast – safe
Typical driver: Businessman

*Citroën Zantia*
Happy with car
Fast – comfortable – music system – good style – colour would
matter (black or red)
Typical driver: Salesman

*Skoda*
Unhappy with car
Make of car has a bad image – bad reputation
Typical driver: Old person

*Mini*
Unhappy with car
Too small – would feel unsafe
Typical driver: First time owner – young person – woman
driver

*Vauxhall Calibra 4 × 4 Turbo*
Happy with car – man's car as it's a 4 × 4 turbo – everything
going for it
Streamlined – stylish – powerful
Typical driver: Young man

*Citroën 2CV*
Wouldn't be bothered with car as it wouldn't fit my image
Budget car
Typical driver: Probation officer – teacher – social worker –
women's car as men wouldn't be happy in it.

After this, the theme that advertising has had a powerful effect
in shaping their attitudes about male power, control and
sexuality is developed. Car adverts are subsequently shown to
the group and analysed. The adverts are placed under the
image headings of 'power and control', 'sex', 'status', and
'fantasy'. Having entered the fantasy world of car advertising,
participants are then taken to the Royal Liverpool Hospital to
see the realities of car use, and the devastation that this inflicts
on both drivers and victims.

## Lessons learnt

Through experience, the COP has evolved to actively
challenge participants' notions of masculinity in relation to
motor vehicles. Lessons have been learnt through emphasising
go-karting as a means of providing a legitimate buzz or
excitement from driving. That session has been replaced by
sessions devoted to 'the image of the car', and its associations
for men as a source of status, power and sexual prowess.
Through debate and discussion with other female
groupworkers, material has been excluded on the grounds of
its macho language or oppressive nature, and we continue to
discuss and debate the relevance of all material used. While the
project continues to offer a two-day course at a local garage,
using qualified mechanics to impart basic skills on MOTs, the
quad and rally biking element of that course has been
removed. The viability of those two days continues to be
explored, and there is a lively question of whether they should
be replaced with drama, video and assertiveness skills. We
remain acutely aware of the dangers of using activities which
might merely validate participants' fascination and obsession
with cars.

The co-ordinators of COP are realists. We know that some
clients will be undeterred from driving. A vital element of our
work has thus centred on attending training days for
magistrates and judges, advising them not to impose
disqualifications from driving when clients appear before the
courts. In our experience, bans from driving have little

deterrent effect in stopping car offenders from driving, and merely have the effect of stopping car offenders from driving legally. The impact of imposing lengthy bans, often up to five years, can lead to the development of fatalistic attitudes, especially with younger offenders, who feel they will never get legal, so, "We might as well drive anyway".

Many clients express the desire to own and drive a car once their ban has ended, and we have accepted the need to link in with local employment training schemes to make this viable. One such scheme offered by NACRO is a course called 'The ABC of Driving', providing a £10 top-up to clients' state benefits. Participants are required to undertake a basic literacy and numeracy course, before being given the opportunity of free driving lessons. Clients are then required to pay for their driving test. In parallel to this, and in response to excessively high insurance premiums often quoted for heavily convicted car offenders, we are establishing links with the Fresh Start scheme run by the National Association of Motor Projects, Sabre Insurance and BSM. The Fresh Start scheme provides third party insurance, over three month renewable periods, whilst discounting all previous motoring convictions. Amongst other criteria, clients are deemed suitable if they have participated in an offending behaviour programme, and then have completed a two day risk awareness driving course run by BSM.

Perhaps the best way of illustrating some of the impact that the programme has had is through the words of the offenders themselves.

> "If I hadn't had the chance to do the COP I'd still be taking cars. Jail makes you worse. Financial penalties are useless if you've got no money in the first place. So if a judge says you have to pay a £200 fine, it's like he's saying go out and rob."

> "The strength of the programme is that it makes you look at everything. I was made up that I wasn't going to prison as my partner was pregnant...it was good timing really cos the COP made me aware of how my family could also be the victims of my stupid mistakes."

> "Going to the hospital was good but hard to do...and all the speakers about victims. They kept whacking you with

stuff. Even though it was uncomfortable, little bits of the programme stick in your head: images, memories. There was one lady there who could have been one of our Ma's. She told us how it hurts her to have her sons locked up. I always think of her.[1]"

## Concluding comments

If masculinity is one of the keys to making sense of car crime, perhaps it is worth asking why women do not figure large. After all, as Pat Carlen (Carlen, 1985) has argued, the study of women and offending is likely to tell us more about how to prevent offending than anything else.

There is a very old and sexist joke about a woman driver believing that the choke was where she hung her handbag. Old and sexist it may be, but it serves to remind us of the impact, and perhaps even the intention of such jokes about women motorists. Their consequence is to obscure the competence and safety records of women motorists and establish that the motor car is very much male territory. Even today, an examination of car adverts, a central part of one of the sessions in COP, indicates that such vehicles are produced primarily for men. They feature men as drivers with women portrayed as a nuisance, or as an admiring audience for male prowess, but rarely as competent drivers or owners, and then only in small and compact cars.

Quite clearly, cars mean very different things to men and women, as the behaviour not only of participants but also of male staff at the go-karting sessions we described above illustrated. In thinking about the value of cars, women tend to identify safety, convenience, reliability and so on. For many men, the car is much more about power, sexuality, freedom and self-esteem. It is not that women do not identify with some of the speed and thrills of motoring, rather that such identification is highly circumscribed for women, who are made conscious that their access to the motor car is with male permission. Women earn less than men; the 'family' car is usually driven by men and, when cars break down, women have to be 'rescued' by male 'knights of the road'. These and a host of other factors make women feel that access to the motor car is, at best, conditional. Moreover, rarely is it central to their femininity. By contrast, for many men, car ownership – or where that is denied, the use of other's cars through illegitimate means – is a central way in which their sense of self is established.

Projects set up to deal specifically with motoring offenders, and indeed courses set up within day centres and client course programmes, are varied in content and may need to be flexible in appearance and structure as patterns of offending change. However, if we accept the basic premise that motoring offending is related to codes of stereotypical masculinity, then questioning these codes and their impact on men needs to be central to the structure of course programmes and projects. Getting groups to tackle basic questions about the gendered nature of motoring is essential.

Often activity has been seen merely as a way of engaging with young people in order to get a particular message home. However, the activity itself may have important lessons to offer. Sessions aimed at learning to care for and maintain machines may breed respect for them. Learning safe as opposed to fast and risky driving may also be effective with some people. However, significant questions seemingly remain about work which involves activities that replicate the speed and excitement – the buzz – of risky driving.

One of the problems with the early history of motor projects, however, has been the tendency to see them as some kind of total solution to the 'problem' they seek to address. The reality, however, is that no project can work without links into other schemes for employment and social skills training, to name but two. A focus on masculinity, though vital, is not enough. Moreover, we cannot expect male offenders to function with a substantially different value system from the rest of the population. Changing public values may seem an impossible task, yet it has been achieved in large measure, for example, in relation to drink driving. Crucially, if the impact of stereotypical masculinities on male behaviours were better acknowledged, we might begin to design even better programmes for those convicted of such offences and, by developing an understanding of 'what works' and with whom, we would be able to target the resources we have available. Until then, no doubt, those involved in car-related crime will continue to drive us crazy.

## References

Briggs, J. (1992) 'Profile of the juvenile joyrider', in *Car Crime: An Accelerating Problem*, Report of the 1992 NAPO Northumbria Branch Conference.

Buckley, K. (1995) 'Masculinity, the probation service and the causes of offending behaviour', in May, T. and Vass, A. (eds.) *Working With Offenders*, London: Sage.

Carlen, P. (1985) (ed.) *Criminal Women*, Oxford: Polity.

Corbett, C. and Simon, F. (1992) 'Decisions to break or adhere to the rules of the road viewed from the rational choice perspective', *British Journal of Criminology* Vol. 32, No. 4, Autumn.

Goldson, B. (1995) *Challenging car crime in the community: An initial evaluation of the Merseyside Probation Service Car Offender Project*, University of Liverpool: unpublished manuscript.

Jackson, D. 1992) 'Riding for joy', *Achilles Heel*, Summer.

Light, R., Nee, C. and Ingham, H. (1993) *Car Theft: The offender's perspective*, Home Office Research Study No. 130, London: HMSO.

Martin, J. P. and Webster, D. (1994) *Probation Motor Projects in England and Wales*, Home Office Publications Unit.

Mayhew, P. and Maung, N. A. (1992) *Surveying Crime: Findings from the 1992 British Crime Survey*, Home Office Research and Statistics Department. Findings No. 2: London: Home Office.

Moore, R. and Lloyd, G. (1992) 'Looking beyond banger racing', *Youth Social Work*, Summer.

The author would like to thank Steve Pimblett whose work formed the basis for some of the description of the COP's programme.

1.    All quotes are taken from Goldson, B. (1995).

# CHAPTER 5

# MEN AND OFFENDING GROUPS

## Kevin Murphy

### Introduction

Since Autumn 1992 male probation staff at the Camberwell Probation Centre have been running 'Men and Offending' groups. More recently groups have been co-run with staff in a prison, a drug agency and a centre for men under 21 years. In all, some 20 groups have met, the majority at Camberwell Probation Centre. This chapter provides an account of our experiences, outlines the background to the group, its relevance to probation work, and some of the key concepts and aims of the group. It will also address anti-discrimination issues, provide details of selected sessions and present some of the results of evaluative studies of the group.

### Background

Interest in addressing issues in relation to men and offending stems from several sources. There has been an increasing awareness and emphasis on anti-discriminatory work within the probation service in recent years. Gender awareness and anti-sexism training has become more commonplace, giving rise to an examination of the range of roles, expectations, behaviour and opportunities which exist for women and men. Real changes affecting structural, economic, social, educational and employment opportunities are taking place, and having a significant impact on the lives of women and men. These changes challenge men to think about their roles, and to examine their assumptions, about themselves and others, which affect their attitudes and behaviour.

For some men this has meant a reaffirmation and

entrenchment of attitudes and behaviour, for others it has led to an uncomfortable, sometimes painful, process of self-examination leading to change. On the personal level I have had opportunities, mainly within the context of my work, to examine some of my attitudes and behaviour and to reflect upon how I have experienced the processes of male socialisation. I believe it is up to individual men to take the responsibility to question, examine and change not only their own attitudes and behaviour, but to do this with other men, particularly when one considers the extent of the damage men cause to themselves and others.

There were three key factors which encouraged the development of the Men and Offending Group: training, opportunity and supervision. In Autumn 1992 three male probation officers from Camberwell Probation Centre attended a two-day training course, 'Masculinity and Offending' run by Trefor Lloyd, a freelance trainer and consultant (see Chapter 9). Within a couple of weeks we had the opportunity to start our first group and had access to Trefor as supervisor for several groups.

### Camberwell Probation Centre

The Camberwell Probation Centre provides the courts with a community sentencing option which is an additional condition of a Probation Order. It consists of a condition of attendance for up to 60 days, and therefore involves a considerable restriction of liberty. The target client group is made up of persistent male offenders aged over 21 years. It is a non-residential programme lasting 40 days. It offers 30 half-day sessions of a 'Reasoning and Rehabilitation Programme' which is a cognitive behavioural programme designed to develop a range of thinking and behavioural skills taught within a structured framework. Sessions cover problem solving, social skills, assertiveness, negotiation skills, managment of emotions, creative thinking, values enhancement and critical reasoning. A similar number of craft sessions are provided, designed to develop creative expression, practical skills and improve self-esteem. There are six sessions with an 'Education, Training and Employment' Group. For black clients, there are 12 sessions of a 'Black Empowerment' group and for white clients 12 sessions of a 'Men and Offending' group. Attendance at all the groups is compulsory.

## Promoting the group

For some men, the idea of attending a Men and Offending group may seem somewhat strange and cause them to feel anxious, prompting questions like, "Do I have to hug trees and beat drums?" We tell the men about the group when they attend for assessment, as they start at the centre, and at the start of the Men and Offending group. We use several 'hooks' to raise interest and allay fears. We ask men to consider why we have a prison population of about 2,000 women and 50,000 men? Are men that much more criminal than women? Why is gender so closely associated with criminality? We explain that the group is designed to allow them to do something that they probably haven't done before: to talk to other men in an all male group about being men. Often when we ask men, "When was the last time you thought about being a man?" there is a blank, surprised look, and a reply along the lines of, "Well, you don't; that's what you are, so what's there to think about?"

## Aims of the Men and Offending group at Camberwell Probation Centre

1) For men to reflect upon being men with other men.

2) For men to examine the messages and expectations they have experienced; to consider the impact of male socialisation on their attitudes and behaviour; to examine how this process links with their offending and how their choices may have been constrained.

3) For men to complete the group with an increased level of awareness of the impact of male socialisation on them and others; to have reconsidered some of their attitudes and behaviour and to be in a better position to consider a wider range of choices affecting their relationships with others and their behaviour as men.

## Key themes for the group

In the Men and Offending group the main theory underpinning our understanding of the way men develop is that of masculine socilisation. From this position masculinity is viewed as being socially constructed. Although biological factors exist, we do not focus on them as significant factors. Men grow up in society where the main message they receive is that being 'male' is the norm. It is a patriarchal society where men have traditionally had access to the institutions, structures and systems which give them power, dominance and influence, which ensure the messages received by men are designed to maintain the status quo. Boys grow up absorbing powerful messages about society being male-dominated in different ways: imitation, observation, through media messages, role models and from their fathers, other men and peers. Developing a male identity is a complex process of socialised learning. It is so much of an established norming process that few men reflect upon the process or are even aware of it. Masculinity is not fixed, it develops over time and there are different masculinities which are shaped by a range of factors, including class, culture and race.

When a baby is born one of the first questions asked is, "What sex is it?" Once this is established the baby will commence the process of being socialised according to gender. As a baby boy grows up through childhood, teenage years to adult man, he will have learned to narrow and limit his behaviour, outlook and attitudes according to expectations and experiences specific to his gender. The process of defining himself according to male identity and belonging, involves distancing from behaviours perceived as different, for instance, anything characterised as female, by hiding emotions and by putting on a public front. In Session three of the group programme we use a model which graphically demonstrates the process and the behavioural changes involved as a young child becomes an adult male.

The process of socialisation during teenage years is particularly intense. The range of acceptable male behaviours is limited; young men learn to restrict the ways they communicate with other young men by using banter and 'piss taking'. Activities are the main focus of attention and energy, the expression of anything but a narrow range of emotions becomes taboo. Establishing a pecking order, finding a role, belonging in terms of group activities, are all important. A lot of offending by young males involves elements of bravado and of putting on a front: it tends to be loud, public, and designed to impress.

A key theme of the group is that of **proving**, which is about how men learn to prove, to themselves and others, that they are developing from being a boy to adult male. Although there are costs in terms of expectations and limitations, there are also significant rewards. Fear of the consequences of being unable to prove belonging is a significant factor and major motivating force. Part of the proving process is to stress **commonality** and deny or distance **difference**. Other groups, for example women, are ascribed particular characteristics and become easy targets which serve to strengthen the bonds of commonality.

The notions of commonality and difference are central themes throughout the group. We aim to provide a safe structure to enable men to explore differences between each other, between men in general and other individuals and groups. We discuss **coping** mechanisms and techniques which men have developed as a means of proving and demonstrating commonality.

We focus on how men cope in public settings such as school and prison. How men behave and what they show of their emotions in public settings is significantly shaped by their gender identity through socialisation. There is often a tension between the **public** front and **private** feelings and emotions, particularly in the company of other men. The showing of emotions, feelings, uncertainty, stress and vulnerability is perceived as weakness, and is devalued as being different. Men therefore have to juggle with this internal tension, often denying emotions and feelings which are overshadowed by the pressures of the public front.

By asking the questions, "What did you do?" and, "How did you feel?", the tensions between public and private can be explored. An all-male group allows men to talk about their experiences of vulnerability, dependence and emotionality which are often hidden by the **public** front. It is important for men to hear that other men have similar experiences and feelings, but often no means of acknowledging or expressing them.

In many of the groups men will identify roles such as 'provider', 'parent', 'protector' and having power, as being strong expectations. Work and having money are important to achieving these expectations. Legitimate work is often difficult to obtain, so offending is an option which helps men to achieve some of these expectations. Employment and its rewards provide status, belonging, influence and reinforce male identity. Men are often judged in terms of 'what they do' and 'what they have'; these are activities and possessions rather than other values and behaviours. There are costs for men who rely too heavily on work for self-identity and worth in terms of coping with redundancy or retirement. Current estimates predict that in five years there will be more women in employment in the UK than men. The significance of changes in working patterns, along with women outperforming men in education, presents a major challenge to male identities. Very few jobs remain which require the traditional male brawn!

It seems important that, given these realities which are particularly heightened for men attending the group, it is essential to help them re-examine the components of male identity, to question its limitations and to explore other values and activities. For example, many of the men appear to have a history of unsuccessful relationships where quality contact with their children, although desired, is often patchy or inadequate. What needs to be challenged is the assumption that men's usefulness as fathers is only in financial or work terms. Men need to develop male identities which broaden the notion of fatherhood away from provider to incorporate emotional, caring and other 'less male' aspects. For some men, limited by the impact of factors such as class, race, criminal record, low self-esteem, few opportunities and poor educational experiences, the sense of 'redundant man' looms large. 'Redundant man' can easily become 'angry man' who copes by denying emotions, by reinforcing male identity and by excessive use of drink and drugs. Aggression towards self and others is often close to the surface. This is manifest in offending, which is why it is central to our work to examine as workers, and with our clients, the limitations and effects of male socialisation, and to encourage men to develop other aspects of male identity.

There are considerable costs for men in the way that central to male identity is the repression/denial to self and others of emotions. It is seen as unmanly and weak to show vulnerability. Many will often say that it is easier to talk about private feelings with women than with men, highlighting the way language is gender defined. Emotions acceptable to male identity tend to be around aggression and humour, often based on competition, which has an element of beating, proving and putting others down. It is sadly not uncommon for men in the group to admit that they do not know how they feel. Feelings are locked away, denied and dealt with indirectly, often in ways that can damage the individual and others. Men's lack of recognition of feelings makes it difficult to acknowledge the feelings of others, thus rendering it easier to offend in the absence of empathy.

Another cost of the limitations of expressing emotions between men is that for most men communication with almost half of the population is restricted, and this seems a great loss and sadness. It is interesting to note that during the recent anniversaries of the ending of the Second World War, there seemed to be a greater willingness from those involved in the war to express emotional reflection, compared to the usual limitations of the public stiff upper lip, "It's a man's duty", silent heroes. For men to develop the confidence to question and develop male identity, there is a need to find ways to think and communicate using language which incorporates emotionality.

By doing this, men can begin to broaden male identity and model it for their sons and other men. The benefits of this are not only for men, but for other groups currently perceived as being different and having less value. In recent decades there have been significant changes affecting the lives of women and, although different women have benefited to varying degrees, these changes have shaped a climate which raises questions about the traditional roles and relationships between men and women. As a consequence, men are being challenged to examine the components of traditional male identity which in part objectifies and belittles women and others perceived as different. Men need to learn to find language and behaviours which reduce the need to compete and gain dominance, but which relies on co-operation, empathy and expression of emotions. As men find different ways to value themselves, the more they will be able to value others.

## Anti-discriminatory issues

The Men and Offending groups at Camberwell Probation Centre, and in the prison, have been made up of white men. Groups at a drug agency and probation centre for men under 21 years have included mixed black and white members and leaders. Making the groups feel safe enough for the men to participate is of primary importance. At the Camberwell Probation Centre we have an introductory 'Anti-Discriminatory Issues' session when men start at the centre.

This is designed to address issues relating to discrimination in behaviour and language. The Inner London Probation Service has a clear equal opportunities policy which is discussed with all group members. We establish ground rules in the groups, and leaders challenge men to consider their language and behaviour.

Unless a man discloses, there tends to be a general assumption made by men in the group that everyone is heterosexual. Our experience is that younger men tend to be the most vocal and intolerant of homosexuality. This may be because homosexuality can present a major 'threat' to their developing sexuality, as it is reinforced by the influences of male socialisation.

There is a fine line between asking members for their views about different groups such as women, gay men and black people, and the point at which the expression of such views becomes insulting or disrespectful. Views that are expressed which we would question are challenged by looking at the way processes of male socialisation have shaped views, and also by attempting to unpick fact from opinion. We ask men to reflect on the differences between intent and effect in terms of language and behaviour. Language which is disrespectful and puts other people down is not acceptable and is challenged. It is easier to become a target or a victim if you are seen as a stereotype rather than as an individual.

Anti-discriminatory practice is increasingly under attack, whether it is in relation to social work training or dismissed and negated by the term 'political correctness'. In the context of the Men and Offending group it is particularly important because these men are socialised to learn that those who are different have less value. The real consequences of this process can be seen in terms of the black, gay and female victims of male offending. Challenging the ways in which men develop attitudes and assumptions about the value of others is essential and consistent with the aims of the probation service in terms of protection of the public, rehabilitation and reducing the risk of re-offending.

### Starting the group

We have found it useful to look at information that may be available in probation files before starting the group, in order to get an overall picture of the men in the group and the possible areas of commonality and difference. Information such as age, living situations, relationships, levels of isolation, responsibilities, problems, patterns of offending and sentencing experiences is useful. This information helps us to tailor the structure and focus of particular sessions. The groups are closed groups in that no newcomers join after Session One and men are expected to attend for the whole period. Sessions last for two and a half hours with half an hour break. We have found that twice weekly sessions provide a good momentum and encourage continuity.

It is important to discuss the role of the group leaders with the group. We concentrate on the fact that although we have roles, such as providing session structure and boundary setting, we are part of the group in that, as men, we have also been subjected to male socialization. As leaders, we participate in all of the exercises and discussions. We emphasise that our role is about doing **with** the group rather than **to** the group.

### Summary of masculinity and offending sessions

1.  Introduction – aims – ground rules – roles of leaders. Agree – discussion statement exercise.

2.  Expectations of men – public heroes – private heroes (people who are respected) – qualities of those respected.

3.  "When did I become a man?" Transition process, young person – adult male. 'Proving' to self and others.

4.  Transition process, dependent – interdependent – roles in teenage groups. Belonging. Commonality and difference affecting attitudes and behaviour.

5.  'Ways men learn to cope' in school, prison. Tensions between public actions and private thoughts and feelings. Basic transactional analysis – ego states and life positions/scripts.

6.  Male image photopack exercises dealing with male power, identity and feelings. Emotion cards. "What did I do the last time I felt… (a particular emotion)."

7.  Benefits of offending.

8.  Costs of offending.

9.  Impact of social class on men.

10.   Challenging racism.

11.   Challenging sexism.

12.   Review of group and evaluation.

Sessions 9, 10, 11 have been added to the Camberwell
Probation Centre groups. The core sessions are 1 – 8 for Men
and Offending, Sessions 1 – 6 are the essential building blocks
for the process of reflection. Other sessions after 1 to 6 can be
developed to address other specific themes such as
Anger/Violence – Drug/Alcohol use – Health – Parenting –
Use of Time – Change – Sexuality – Homophobia –
Relationships – according to the needs of a particular group.

The groups in the prison seem to have worked well as an initial
group for men to reflect on attitudes and behaviour. It has
resulted in them being able to make a better self-assessment
and commitment to subsequent groups designed to address
specific behaviours, for instance, anger management, sex
offender treatment programmes and relationships groups. The
advantages of undertaking a Men and Offending group in a
prison setting are that the men are in an environment which
encourages reflection and some of the themes discussed in the
group, such as the tension between public behaviour and
private thoughts and feelings along with coping strategies, are
very real issues.

We have found that adjustments needed to be made to the
group when working with younger men and teenagers. We
shorten the session length, introduce a wider range of methods
to stimulate the group, e.g. videos, magazines, games and
photos, and reframe some of the questions to make them more
relevant to the group. Although teenage men are going
through the process of becoming men, the groups are able ro
reflect on how they are affected by the process.

For the purpose of this chapter I have selected three sessions to
describe in detail – sessions two, three and four.

### Session two

**Aims**

The aims of this session are to recap on the previous session:
  • To identify and discuss what men are expected to be in

terms of roles, stereotypes and images.

- To consider the consequences of these expectations.
- To identify public heroes.
- To identify those people they respect (private heroes/heroines) and to highlight their qualities and characteristics.
- To compare these to those of public heroes and to the list of male expectations.
- To evaluate the session.

**Methods**

We ask the question, "What are men expected to be?" and list responses. We encourage the group to think about images, roles, the media, relationships, activities, stereotypes and behaviour. The following is a typical list:

Breadwinner, to set example, fighter, provider, responsible, capable, unemotional, good at DIY, be in control, bottle things up, sexually active, tough, reliable, loving, have power, control family, humorous, independent, cry alone, good at sport, punishers (of children), drinker, schemer, competitive, macho, to have money, be successful, to take it like a man.

In one group a member took the pen unprompted and wrote 'Superman' at the top of the list. For some, the list can seem overwhelming. We guide discussion to address the following points:

- What do they think about the range of expectations?
- Where do they come from and on what are they based?
- Can any one man live up to all these expectations?
- Do expectations change – do some conflict?
- How realistic are these expectations?
- How do men cope with these expectations?
- What happens and how does it feel if you cannot, or choose not to, live up to some of these expectations?

Each man is asked to choose two expectations from the list

which are important to him; these can be expectations he is already undertaking or would like to fulfil. This allows men to put down 'personal' markers within a 'public' exercise. By circling those chosen on the flipchart, a picture of commonality and difference in the group emerges.

We continue by asking, "Who were/are your heroes?"

Usually a long list emerges reflecting different ages and interests. We concentrate on the 'public' heroes, asking the group to think about the heroes they imitated and perhaps dreamed of becoming. Usually the list covers heroes from films, music, entertainment, sports, crime and politics.

We guide discussion to cover:

- Is the range of heroes fairly narrow?

- How do/did we relate to our heroes? Can we recall anecdotes?

- Are there links between the heroes as stereotypes and the expectations of men identified earlier in the session?

- What did/do we like about our heroes?

- How have they influenced us?

We acknowledge that we have asked a gender-specific question and ask about heroines or any 'public' women who have influenced them. Often women identified are typically entertainers, sex symbols and, occasionally, the saintly. We ask the group to reflect on heroines in the same way as we did for heroes, drawing out similarities and differences.

During the course of the heroes/heroines exercise men often identify 'personal' heroes and heroines. We discuss them in the next part of the session by asking, "Who do you respect?" We list these individuals; there are usually equal numbers of women and men. We then ask, "What is it about each person that you respect/value?" We list the various qualities and characteristics. A typical list is: being there for me; listened to me; gave me confidence; looked after me; helped; showed tenderness; stood by me; valued me; respected me; was fair and balanced; gave me encouragement; spent time with me.

We discuss these qualities and stress that if men in the group value these qualities in others, it is likely that they recognise and value the same qualities in themselves. We compare these qualities with the stereotypes in the lists from the 'heroes' and 'expectations of men' exercises earlier in the session. Men in the group are often taken aback by the extent of the contrast. The session ends with **evaluation**. The method we use is to ask each man to rank 0–10 the following questions:

- How interesting did you find the session?
- Did it make you think?
- How comfortable did you feel with today's ideas?
- How comfortable did you feel with others in the group?
- How comfortable did you feel with the leaders?
- Any comments?

The forms can be completed anonymously and provide instant feedback to the group leaders so that any concerns raised can be discussed in preparing for the next session.

The group leaders should meet between sessions to evaluate and prepare. By asking ourselves, "How did each man participate?" we have found this to be a good initial question. Group dynamics and the co-working relationship should also be discussed.

## Session three

### Aims

The aim of this session, after recapping on the previous session, is to explore aspects of the process of becoming a man. We introduce the idea that being a man is a key part of our identity, shaping how we view ourselves and others, and also how we are viewed. Male identity is important, but little attention is paid to the process of becoming a man. We aim to enable men to reflect upon their experiences and those of others, and to consider the nature of the process of becoming a man.

### Methods

We ask the group to think about, "When did I become a man?" Initially we listed answers, but we now start by using prepared cards each marked with a different answer to the question, and drawn from answers provided by previous groups. The advantage of this is that it allows the group to consider a very wide range of answers and each group can add new cards.

The following is a selection of the answers on cards to the above question: when I left care; when adults started to ask me for advice; when I became a dad; when I started to work; when someone close to me died; when I started drinking in pubs; when I began to claim the dole; when I first had sex with someone else; when I reached a certain age; when I started to behave as an adult; when I began to drive; when I caught my first trout (relates to being taught by his father to catch trout by tickling them); it's still happening; when I started to serve adult prison sentences; when I first got tattooed; when I first had to look after myself.

Most men will say that they have not thought about this question before, and some are surprised at the range of events and incidents. We guide discussion so that the men reflect upon the following points:

- Whether there are definite events or incidents to indicate when you become a man?
- What are the feelings associated with particular events?
- Is there a difference between when you feel you are a man and when other people treat you as a man?
- How were you treated by others and what was expected of you?
- How did you prove to yourself and others that you were becoming a man?
- Has becoming a man been a different process for men from previous generations and different cultures? If so, what has been different?
- How much of the process of becoming a man is about being accepted, having a sense of belonging and recognition by other men?

We make the point that becoming a man is an individual process, with a social context which men experience differentially involving a range of events, incidents, actions and feelings. It is a powerful process which is rarely thought about or discussed.

We move on to look at the process in more detail in an exercise we have come to call 'Matchstick Man'. On a flipchart we draw a matchstick man outline and on the left hand side write YOUNG. We ask the group to list characteristics associated with young people – for example, 7, 8, 9, 10 year-olds. What do they do? What are they like? What are they expected or allowed to be? Often the following characteristics emerge: creative; small; happy; playful; free; get things wrong; impressionable; innocent; energetic; trusting; vulnerable; protected; learning; no worries; open; dependent; show emotions.

On the right hand side we write: ADULT MEN, those of 18 plus years, and in a similar way ask the group for characteristics and expectations. Often the following emerge: know it all; worker; sexually experienced; tough; be in a relationship; a boozer; be responsible; not show feelings; be in control; have money; be stable; able to cope; independent; stand up for himself; hide emotions; be an expert; be in charge; be experienced; large; a provider. We ask the group to reflect on the two lists, and guide discussion to address the following points:

- Which list is more attractive?

- How do men move from YOUNG to ADULT MALE?

- What happens to those characteristics not transferred from young? Are they lost, repressed, or do they become dormant?

- How do men know when they have completed the process?

We ask for recollections of the transition process in terms of anecdotes about activities and feelings. We point out the characteristics under **young** usually apply equally to girls and boys. We introduce the concept of **proving** as a key part of the process of becoming a man. We ask men to consider ways that they prove to themselves and others that they are going through, or have gone through, the process of becoming a man. This concept is revised in the next session. The session ends with an evaluation.

## Session four

### Aims

The aims of this session are to explain and to develop the themes raised in the previous session in relation to the process of becoming a man.

- To reinforce the idea of **proving** to self and others.

- To identify the ways in which behaviour choices tend to become narrower as a boy becomes an adult man.

- To examine the above by focusing on the roles and dynamics of teenage groups.

### Methods

Recap from the previous session, highlighting the proving to self and others that shapes the process of becoming a man. Refer to the list under ADULT MEN from the 'Matchstick Man' exercise and discuss the extent to which the range of behavioural choices becomes narrow. What impact has the narrowing had on their lives? How do men learn to fit into the limited range of adult male behaviour? What consequences does this process have for others?

Introduce the idea that the process is in part reflected by a shift from: YOUNG **DEPENDENT** to ADULT **INDEPENDENT** which usually comes from the Matchstick Man exercise. Ask the group to consider what 'Independent' means. Have they achieved independence? Can any one man be truly independent and what are the pressures involved in being independent? After some discussion suggest **'interdependence'** as a more realistic goal. This allows men to acknowledge they may have retained an element of dependency and this can, for some, be a liberating concept. Highlight roles and needs which involve elements of dependency such as to be loved, having others to love, to be cared for, having others to care about, the need for comfort and security, a desire to value self and be valued by others. Link these often unacknowledged aspects to the qualities possessed by those identified in Session two from the 'respect' exercise.

Return to the process of the development of male identity and consider how individuals make the transition to adult men.

Head a flipchart sheet **'roles in teenage groups'** and draw a large circle. Ask the group to identify roles that young men play in teenage groups. Point out that these groups can be formal or informal, of varying size and duration. The following roles commonly emerge: leader; moneybags/banker; nutter; risktaker; romeo; fighter; joker; organiser; stirrer; boozer; piss-taker; sensible; follower; ponce; show-off; dreamer; wheelsman; scapegoat; boaster; rebel; eccentric; planner.

As the list is being compiled, we ask the group for anecdotes. What did these characters do? What were they like? How did they relate to each other? Guide discussion to reflect the following issues:

- Ask about belonging to the group in terms of joining, getting accepted and leaving.

- How were people seen as differently treated?

- How important was it to belong to a group and why was it important?

- Within the group was there tension between public behaviour and private feelings and emotions?

- What sort of rules did the group have?

- Was the range of behaviour and expression of attitudes narrow?

- Was the group a way of **proving** to self and others about becoming a man?

- How much of the attraction to belong was motivated by the fear of not belonging, of not being accepted and thus leading to rejection by other men?

Being part of a teenage group meets a variety of needs and for many is central to the process of becoming a man. As the group discusses anecdotes several points can be made to help the group reflect upon the meaning of various activities.

How young men communicate is important in that **banter** and **piss-taking** are significant features. This type of communication serves as a way of including and identifying those who belong and as a means of distancing and devaluing those who are different. Such language teaches young men to avoid the use of more private emotional language. The language tends to be about activities, behaviour and public attitudes. How men learn to talk to one another as teenagers tends to set the pattern for their adult years. It has the overall effect of limiting communication between men to the extent that the expression of a large range of emotions, feelings and vulnerabilities becomes taboo. We ask whether men in the group think the way they talk to other men is limited?

Activities in male teenage groups often have **proving** as a major motivation. This is manifested by competing, obtaining status and respect, establishing a place in the pecking order, testing boundaries, being daring and taking risks. Discussion about offences committed by teenage males is likely to highlight these factors, for instance, criminal damage, offences associated with excessive drinking, auto offences, public fighting offences, and acquisitive offences which provide the means to enhance image and status.

Belonging, and the emphasising of commonality in teenage groups, is achieved by the importance given to fashions, clothing and appearance. Music also serves as a means of establishing common identity. We ask the group about what they wore, what they looked like, and reflect on the importance of appearance in terms of identification and belonging.

Another way of establishing commonality and group identity is the status given to events and incidents which provide group folklore and strengthen continuity. For instance, the post mortem in the pub the following day about what happened the night before, the excitement of did you see, were you there, what was your role, and what happened, become tales that are repeated and often exaggerated. Strength, daring, risk-taking and other status elements are woven into the telling of the tales.

In male teenage groups, characteristics associated with being a man are learnt, practised, reinforced and become valued. Characteristics associated with difference, such as some of those on the YOUNG side of the 'Matchstick Man' exercise, Session three, are devalued. Individuals and groups who are seen as being different are devalued. Not only do they become easy potential targets or victims, but the process of targeting and victimising serves to strengthen the commonality of the group. This can be illustrated by drawing each letter of OLDER in five boxes:

O L D E R    **FEMALE/GAY**

decreasing in size to reflect the narrowing of the range of behaviours expected as a man. By putting Female and Gay outside the last box it denotes those groups who are typically devalued because they are different. We ask the group to identify other individuals and groups who were devalued as outsiders, e.g. grasses, swots, boffins, nerds, train spotters, unattractive people. We ask how they think these people feel about being devalued? It is not uncommon to have someone in the group who has been an outsider, and it is important to encourage him to relate how he coped and felt.

Returning to the list of teenage roles, we ask each man to identify and circle two roles they played as teenagers. We repeat this by asking for two roles that they consider they currently play in groups particularly with other men. Next:

- Reflect whether the roles identified for each man are similar or different between then and now?

- Have some men become stuck in roles, either then or now?

- Do men wish they could change the roles played, then and now?

- What stops them changing? Is it pressure from self/others?

- Can men identify links or some continuity between roles learned, practised and reinforced as a teenager and roles they play now?

- How much choice do men feel they have about the roles played?

- To what extent have they conformed to, or rebelled against, the roles and expectations?

We acknowledge that the processes discussed in these sessions are often very powerful influences which shape how each man comes to see himself. There are benefits and costs as a result of these processes. By reflecting upon them men can become better-informed about how they have come to see themselves.

They can question the extent to which each man is shaped as a consequence of a social learning process and whether this gives room to question and reconsider attitudes and behaviour.

The session ends with an evaluation.

### Evaluation of the Men and Offending programme

There have been two evaluations of the Men and Offending programme. The first was undertaken by Inner London Probation Service Research and Intelligence Unit and was based on Exit Evaluation Forms completed by means of an interview. The following quotes are taken from the exit evaluations of a sample of men who attended Men and Offending group in late 1994.

> "It increased my knowledge of what men are expected to do because of generations before."

> "Really good on roots of offending, where it all starts."

> "We had a good debate on whether you are born or become an offender."

> "I got a lot of things out that I'd bottled up – it gets a hell of a lot off your chest."

The second evaluation was undertaken by a senior probation officer who had experience of the first seven programmes at the centre. She developed two questionnaires to examine attitude-shifts and self-evaluation of abilities. She concluded that, "The Men and Offending groups appear to have an impact upon men's attitudes and seem to be of particular benefit if conducted in a closed environment like a prison. Men's views were more moderate and considered than expected. The degree of importance these men attributed to feelings and sensitivity was higher than expected. We can speculate that men's public views, which may well conform to stereotypes, are not indicative of their private views. This sort of group allows men the space to consider alternatives and question the expectation to conform to restrictive norms, and therefore give themselves choices about their behaviour which can only be of positive value."

She also wrote the following summary based on her qualitative evaluation of the first seven groups.

"This is a relatively new way of engaging male offenders in probation and reflects an increasing awareness of the importance of gender socialisation in offending. Evaluation of the groups to date shows that it is a very effective way of engaging male offenders and helping them to develop self-awareness through reflection and self-questioning."

"The need for an all-male group to conduct this type of work might be seen by some as controversial, in running the risk of collusion between leaders and participants. In the case of these groups, the leaders had extensive access to consultancy, had undergone gender awareness training, and had had the involvement of women as supervisors and evaluators..."

"Some of the content of the group could be adapted for use in one-to-one work and this basis could probably be used to good effect by both female and male workers, as long as a questioning rather than challenging style was employed. Certainly the basic tenets underpinning this work would be of value to any worker in enhancing her or his understanding of male behaviour."

# CHAPTER 6

# WORKING WITH MEN WITH VIOLENT PATTERNS

## Luke Daniels

### Introduction

Counselling men to stop their violence is a relatively new idea.
Much of the pioneering work began in the USA and continued
later in Canada. Work in Britain, however, remains on a
relatively small scale. There are, for example, no centres in
Wales; Scotland has one established and there is the prospect
of a few new ones opening soon. In England there are five at
the most, with the Everyman Centre – where the work
discussed in this chapter was based – being the largest. Over
the past five years we have seen over 600 men. We now have a
waiting list of at least 100 men, and at times we have had to
close the list as waiting could take six months or more.

There has been much debate about the usefulness of 'working'
with men for change. Some women's groups in particular are
opposed to work with men on two main grounds. First, that it
simply does not work and, second, because it will deflect
money away from work with women. The first is based on the
argument that there is some research which suggests that work
with violent men does not result in changed attitudes to
violence. There are, of course, various models of working with
violent men, and some are more successful than others.
Recently, Dale Hurst, a psychologist working with violent men
in Australia was commissioned to investigate the different
models and ways of working with men all over the world. He
stopped at the Everyman Centre on his way back from the
USA and reported that the models he felt were most successful
were those that had a therapeutic and educational input – very

much the way we at the Everyman Centre approached our work with men.

The second argument – that work with men will divert money from women's projects – is something we have been conscious of at the Everyman. We have been deliberate in where we ask for funding. We have never been adequately funded and receive but a fraction of the funding that some women's groups receive. Having refuges for women is a help to our work, as often it is important that there is a separation of partners while we work with men. It ought to be the case that services are provided for men, without this adversely affecting women's groups, and it is certainly divisive to argue over resources.

### The counsellor

It is important that men take responsibility for their violence if they are to change their violent behaviour. The counsellor must make it a priority to see that the client is doing this before any progress can be made. The counsellor must first work on his own experiences of violence if he is to be an effective counsellor for men.

With the counselling of violent men still being a relatively new initiative in the UK, most of the existing centres have adopted their approach from North American models. The Everyman Centre is different from other centres in that we have not adopted any model, and we also see men who have been violent to other men. We also have different approaches in counselling men within the centre. There is a psychotherapeutic approach, one loosely based on a cognitive analytical therapy approach. I work with an approach loosely based on co-counselling, but developed out of the experience of working with violent men over the years. The work with men that I will describe in this chapter is the programme as it has stood for the last year. It is likely to change as I try new methods and adopt things that seem to work with the men.

### The general approach to work with men

Although we have different approaches we are agreed on some fundamental principles. First, 'responsibility'. We believe that each man must take responsibility for his violence if he is to change his behaviour. It is important that we challenge any notions of, "She made me do it". Second, a belief that men 'can change' their behaviour. At the Everyman Centre we run a six month course in two parts lasting 12 weeks each.

### Individual sessions

These sessions, lasting one hour per week, will give the counsellor the opportunity to work with the client on accepting his responsibility for his violence. The counsellor will also have the opportunity to explore where the violent patterns of behaviour were learned. Often the client would have learnt these patterns in early childhood, most would have been hit and many would have seen violence done to their mothers. In these sessions I have discovered that most men will try to disregard the violence that was done to them as children as, "Nothing more than we deserved". This has parallels with some of their explanations of their partners "deserving" a beating. I encourage the men to remember how they felt when they were being mistreated. Sometimes they will break down in tears as they recount their mistreatment to me. I encourage this show of feelings as it helps them to reclaim their ability to show empathy. The counsellor has to be able to strike the right balance here in challenging their violent behaviour, whilst at the same time giving men the safety they need to show their feelings. Most men with violent patterns have been badly neglected or beaten when young and need some sympathy for their mistreatment if they are to recover and lead non-violent lives.

### Groupwork

Twelve sessions lasting two hours once a week gives men the opportunity to share their experiences and get support for changing their behaviour. The groupwork is both therapeutic and educational. Now that they have accepted responsibility for their violence, it is time to move on to consciousness-raising experience. Much of men's violence to women is a result of the sexist notions they have of women. There are many other issues involved in why men behave violently and I try to cover as many as I can over the 12 weeks. I will describe these in separate sections. The groupwork is structured, but with some flexibility.

I often counsel men in front of the group and it is not unusual for men to show their feelings when I am working with them. Naturally, at the beginning they are very nervous about what to expect, but they soon relax and look forward to the sessions.

Many want to continue with the support they have received and they join an 'ongoing' group. My ideal group size is 12 men, excluding me and an assistant. Sometimes there are fewer men.

Apart from the awareness raising and the counselling, I think the most useful thing I do is to teach the men some basic counselling skills, drawing on my co-counselling background. Men feel that they are more able to talk about how they feel and become better listeners. I encourage men to think about their feelings and, therefore, each group begins with a question about feelings. At the end of each session we hold hands in a circle while we take turns at answering the questions at the close. Men usually sit on cushions during these sessions.

The format of the group is:

- Opening circle
- Theory
- Questions
- Each-way sessions
- Song
- Feedback
- Speakout
- Sessions
- Closing circle

### Session one: Introductions

The first session is slightly different so I will describe it separately. It should be borne in mind that this is a draft programme.

**Welcome**

I would like to congratulate you for coming this far. Now that you have finished your individual sessions it is time for us to move on. I know it is not easy as we men have been conditioned not to ask for help. That you have come this far is an indication that you are determined to change your behaviour.

I now introduce myself and my assistant does the same.

> Introductions
> Name
> Where travelled from
> How you are feeling

Most of the men would have said that they felt nervous. I now introduce a game to help them to relax and to get them to memorise each other's names. For the group to be a safe and supportive place for change it is important that we have some rules before proceeding. I invite you to think about some rules you would like, here are some I need for the group:

**Rules**

1. **No socialising**. We are here for a specific purpose and to try and add other activities may confuse the issue. Also, for the safety of the group it is important that people do not socialise in any way, as this may undermine the confidence of others in the group. I do not want anyone to meet for any purpose for the duration of the sessions. After the sessions I will encourage you to form supportive relationships, so I ask you to be patient.

2. **Abstinence**. For the process to work well I need people to be here with all of their attention. Addictive substances have the ability to numb the true feelings I will be encouraging people to feel. So I am asking people not to take alcohol or any mood altering drugs for at least 12 hours before coming. If I feel that someone is high, I will exclude them from the group. There will be a no smoking policy for the duration of each class.

3. **Confidentiality**. Anything that is said in the group remains here. I encourage you to be open and honest in the knowledge that no one will repeat anything said here to anyone outside the group, or discuss anything another man may have said with anyone in the group without his permission to do so. It must not be assumed that anything a man discussed in the group process is up for debate without his permission. I will be counselling men in front of the group from time to time. Whatever is disclosed in those sessions is completely confidential.

At this point I will encourage men to come up with some more ground rules. Some they usually come up with are:

4.   **Punctuality**. Be on time for sessions. It is not a good use of time to start late or have me repeat things for latecomers.

5.   **Respect**. That everyone is treated with respect, despite having to perhaps disagree with their views at times.

**The programme**

Now that some ground rules have been established, I will outline the programme. We will be covering a variety of issues that may have influenced your decision to use violence. In your individual sessions you would have learned to take responsibility for your violence and would have had time to look at your personal difficulties. We are now moving on to replacing your past violent behaviour with a new attitude to violence. It is not enough to just give you information so I will be counselling you, as I feel it necessary to do so. However, we have all been miseducated in an oppressive society so I hope this exercise and the information given will raise your consciousness for positive change. These are the issues we will be covering over the 12 weeks:

1.   Welcome, introductions and programme

2.   Men's liberation

3.   Homophobia

4.   Sexism

5.   Racism and internalised racism

6.   Language

7.   Love class

8.   Relationship building

9.   Parenting

10.   Addictions

11.   Goal setting

12.   Endings

Any questions about the programme answered.

Some of the men in the group would have been counselled by other members of staff or by one of our volunteer counsellors in their one-to-one sessions. The others would have been counselled by me and would have an understanding of how I work. I now give a brief explanation of my perspective.

I make the assumption that all men are inherently good. That when we behave in ways that do not reflect that assumption it is as a result of the way we have been mistreated ourselves. None of us would mistreat anyone if we were not mistreated in the first place. This mistreatment could take different forms. For some it will have been severe and would include sexual, psychological and physical abuse, as well as seeing domestic violence. For others it might be the misinformation, neglect, socialisation to violence, and lack of positive role models, to name a few. This mistreatment has left us with many unhealed hurts that cause us to behave badly. If we put some attention on these early hurts and are able to let some feelings about them show (discharge) we will have started the recovery process. At last we start to make sense of our bad behaviour, and by repeatedly reviewing the hurt and discharging it, we will be able to heal and overcome our hurtful behaviour patterns. I will encourage you to notice where you have been hurt and, using my counselling skills, we will be able to start the recovery process by getting some discharge going. How much we will be able to achieve depends on you. I can only assist you to the extent that you want to change.

One of the regular complaints that we get from women is that men do not listen well, or talk about their feelings. Throughout the sessions we will be developing these skills by spending some time talking about our feelings and listening to each other in pairs. Essentially, these are counsellor and client roles. We will now divide into pairs and take turns at listening and talking. We will start with five minutes listening to your partner then five minutes talking to him; each taking turns to talk and listen.

**Song**. A songsheet is provided so everyone can participate. We would generally sing when we are happy. It is good to let people know when we are happy. Most of us got hurt around our voices, when people noticed our voices changing at puberty. It is time to reclaim our singing voices. We will be dealing with some heavy issues and some lightness and fun is necessary so we do not get completely sunk.

**Feedback**. What was it like listening/talking? Did you share this time equally?

**Closing the circle**. Men would now be encouraged to come in closer, to link hands as we sit on cushions to a closing circle. We may discuss feelings, or things to look forward to.

### Session two: Men's liberation

We live in a society that oppresses everyone. We men have not escaped that oppression. In fact, the oppression is so deep and wide for us we often cannot see outside it to recognise it for what it is. Almost every other group can recognise their oppression because usually there is another group doing the oppressing. For example, with anti-semitism it is gentiles who are the oppressors. With the oppression of men it is harder to notice because there is no one group doing the oppressing; we are oppressed by the society as a whole through the culture, economy, political system and actions of individuals or groups. It is important to note that it is not females as a group who are oppressing males but society as a whole.

This oppression starts as soon as we are born. Research shows that we will be treated differently from girl babies; we will be cuddled less and handled more roughly to toughen us up for the roles that will be forced upon us. It is almost universal that we hear 'come on, big boys don't cry'. This has the effect of preventing the healing of ourselves when we are hurt. This interruption of one of the most important ways we heal ourselves is responsible for much of the distress we carry as men. Sometimes we are even beaten if we show feelings at an early age. Later on in life we will be blamed for not being able to show feelings. Added to this mistreatment, we will then be conditioned to play two major roles.

1. **Provider**. We are the ones who are expected to provide for our families. We will often have our manhood judged by how well we provide. The cultural norm for a long time has been that a woman's place is at home, therefore a man's place must be at work. Men have internalised this oppression to the point that if they are not working they feel useless and desperate. Recently, the Samaritans released statistics showing that suicide rates have risen sharply for young men, especially in areas of high unemployment.

2.  **Killers**. We are the ones in time of war who are expected to do the killing for society. Often it will be kill or be killed. The conditioning for this role begins as soon as our sex has been identified. Before we can run we will be given an arsenal of toys to begin the preparation for our life of violence. For role models we will have a number of mega movie stars glorifying violence. These role models will be well rewarded for their violence. Everywhere we look we will see images of violent men. The news and newspapers will be full with stories of the violence that men do. So pervasive is the conditioning that most people think men are violent by nature. As boys we will be encouraged to be tough and will have to learn to fight, or be called names like 'sissy' if we decline. Many of us, on complaining to our fathers that we had been beaten at school or the playground, will be sent back to fight or get a hiding.

- Comments, questions.
- Reminder of listening in pairs skills. Select a man you have not shared time with before. Spend 10 minutes on: (i) what has your socialisation been like, and (ii) the first fight you can remember being involved in.
- Song.
- Feedback.
- Counsel one man on his socialisation to violence in front of the group.
- Closing circle.

### Session three: Homophobia

This is, basically, the fear of getting close to the same sex. The nature of the oppressive society we live in depends on us mistrusting each other as men. Homophobia serves to underpin the oppression of men by keeping us apart. If we were to truly get close as men and talk about how we really feel, that would be a liberating exercise. We may want to change the society we live in and replace it with a more just society. If we men could really care by getting to know each other, we would find it very hard to fight one another. We all have to fight to defend the rights of gay men. How else can we call for the ending of our own oppression? The oppression of gay men has nothing to do with sex. It is to do with daring to be different. Our liberation as men depends on the liberation of gay men.

- Comments, questions.

- Reminder of listening skills. Fifteen minutes each way listening: what were your early childhood friendships with boys like?
- Song.
- Feedback.
- Counsel one man on his homophobia in front of group.
- Speak out on violence by one man.
- Closing circle.

## Session four: Sexism

We live in a society that is saturated in sexism. All men are affected by it. Part of the oppression of men is that we are pushed into the role of being the agents of oppression of women. This oppression is supported by the culture and its institutions. Just over 100 years ago it was legal for a man to beat his wife with a stick providing it was no thicker than his thumb. A woman could not own property or get a loan from the bank. She was denied education and even today her care of children and the family is not counted as work. Everywhere we see the way women's bodies are used as sexual objects for the sale of anything from dishwashers to a garden hose. As the agents of oppression of women we use our violence to keep women in their place. It is in our own interest to put an end to the oppression of women, for as long as we are playing this role we can never be liberated as men. We all get some benefit from this oppression in that women are generally paid less and made to feel inferior to men. However, we would benefit a great deal more from the liberation of women. We can change our behaviour to women because there is nothing in us as men that makes us sexist. It is learnt behaviour from the patriarchal society we live in. With a great deal of effort we can un-learn this behaviour.

- Comments, questions.
- Fifteen minutes each way listening. Questions in handout, for example: What was the sexism like in your family? How were the gender roles played out?
- Song.
- Feedback to group.
- Counsel some men on their sexism.
- Speakout.
- Closing circle.

### Session five: Racism and internalised racism

We live in a society saturated by racism. None of us escape its effects. A study by Hartmann and Husband (1974) shows that in areas without large immigrant populations, children obtained their knowledge, ideas and opinions about immigrants predominantly from the media. As a result of this exposure, black people were seen as causing trouble and conflict; as being a 'social problem' in themselves. Black people have no control over the way they are represented in the press. Over the generations we have been portrayed as being violent, lazy, ignorant, pimps, prostitutes, untrustworthy, idiots and many other negative stereotypes. When portrayed in a positive light, it is usually as sportsmen and women, dancers and singers, thus reinforcing the stereotypes so commonly held about black people.

It is important to note that white people are not inherently racist but they learn to be racist because of the society we live in. Racism, like many of the oppressions, is there as a tool to exploit for economic and other reasons. It could be argued that racism as an ideology in Britain began with the movement of Africans as slaves from Africa to the Caribbean and the Americas. Many groups in Britain objected to this movement as they felt it was morally wrong to treat humans as property. As a result, the slave owners mounted a campaign to convince people that they were doing the Africans a favour by 'civilising' them. In this way a campaign of misinformation about Africans started; that, for example, we were savages and lived in trees. Long after slavery the misinformation continues. Some researchers are even 'discovering' a gene for violence which is, as one might expect, to be found mainly in black people. The ideology of racism has affected all of us; causing white people in some cases to view black people as less intelligent and less valued; causing some black people to feel they are not as good as or as capable as white people. Some of us act out the stereotypes that are harmful to us; that we are violent and we are bad.

- Questions, comments.
- Fifteen minutes each way listening.
  For white men:
  (i) First time you were aware of a black person?
  (ii) What is the racism like in your community/family?
  For black men:
  (i) What was the internalised racism like in your family?
  (ii) How has racism affected your life?

- Song.

- Feedback.

- Counsel someone on giving up racism or internalised racism.

- Speak out on violence.

- Closing circle.
  (i) Something you like about yourself
  (ii) Appreciation for a man in the group.

## Session six: Language

The language we use to describe women and our relationships can make a difference in our attitudes to women. Often we talk about women as if they were objects or possessions: 'my woman'. It may be better to start using a different approach in thinking about the person you are having a relationship with. 'Partner' is now much used and it may be better in that it implies some kind of equality. Often men talk of 'the wife'. Here again the woman is referred to as an object – it is no wonder many men feel that they can do what they like to 'the wife'.

- Questions, comments.

- Group exercise.
  (i) Words used to describe women negatively.
  (ii) Words used to describe men negatively.
  Some discussion of the words used in this exercise.
  (i) Words used to describe women positively.
  (ii) Words used to describe men positively.
  Some discussion of the words used in this exercise.

- Ten minutes each way on:
  (i) The words you most frequently use about your partner.
  (ii) Where did you learn those words?

- Song.

- Feedback.

- Speakout.

- Session in group.

- Closing circle.

## *Session seven: Love class*

Professor Leo Buscaglia, after teaching a love class at the University of Southern California for three years, did not feel able to come up with a definition for love, so we will not attempt one here. However, let's consider what the loving person is like. The loving person is spontaneous. Often we lose the ability to be spontaneous, as society demands that we be regimented. We have forgotten what it is like to act on a good impulse; to buy those flowers, newspaper, sweets or whatever it is that your partner appreciates. The loving person is feeling; but we have forgotten what it is like to have a good laugh and to show our feelings. If we feel something, let's show it. If you feel like laughing, then laugh. If you feel like crying, cry. At first it feels a bit difficult as one of the symptoms of our oppression is the way we have become numbed by the years of not being encouraged to show our feelings. This is where the 'big boys don't cry' really gets us. Then, notice, as is the case with every oppression, how we get blamed for not being able to show feelings. The loving person likes closeness; we are constantly moving away from ourselves and each other. By touching we are sure of the other person's existence and we know that they are alive. Many of us have been hurt by unaware touching as children, and some have been sexually abused. Consequently, we have to be conscious of how we touch. You have been encouraged to hold hands and touch in the group as one way of breaking down the barriers that separate us. We looked at how the oppression of men is underpinned by homophobia (the fear of getting close to each other). We need not be afraid to touch, to feel and to show emotion.

The loving person is one who continually sees the wonder and joy of people, places, birds, trees, of being alive. Buddhists believe in the here and now. If you live for tomorrow, which is only a dream, then all you have is an unrealised dream. The past is no longer real; it has value because it made us what we are now. When you are eating, or when you are making love, catch the beauty of the moment. The loving person has no need to be perfect – only human. Perfection is frightening and we are almost afraid to do anything, because we can't do anything perfectly. In creating we affirm our existence.

Men are always capable of change and growth, and if you don't believe this you are in the process of dying. Everything is in the process of change, including you. Herbert Otto says, "Change and growth take place when a person has risked himself and dared to become involved in experimenting with his life. To do this is very exciting – full of joy – but at the same time very frightening. Frightening because you are dealing with the unknown, shaking complacency." Now that you have decided to give up violence, I encourage you to start loving. To love truly you cannot hate, to give love you must have love in the first place. Unfortunately, love is a learned emotion and most of us have not been taught how to love, but it is never too late to learn. We can begin to reclaim our loving nature by showing appreciation for the people around us.

- Questions, comments.
- Group. Take turns sharing:
  (i) What it was like the first time you fell in love?
  (ii) How do you express your love?
- Song.
- Speakout.
- Session time.
- Closing circle.

### Session eight: Relationship building

Relationships need a great deal of care and attention if they are to grow. Many of us, at the beginning of a relationship give a lot of time and energy to it, but after a comparatively short time we stop giving that level of attention. As a result, a common complaint about men from women is that we do not listen or share our feelings. I argue that the ideal relationship would be one that is unconditional. However, many of us cannot attain this so it would at least be good to be clear about what we want from the relationship. We say, "I love you" and usually it carries with it all kinds of unexpressed conditions. These conditions usually lead to many of the difficulties we face in a relationship. If only we had been clear in the first place there would not be so many upsets. It would be a good idea to find out from your partner what she wants; you say what you want, then you negotiate the difficulties. Of course, it would be best to do this with a skilled counsellor. For those of you still in a relationship, here is a simple exercise you can practise with your partner if she agrees; you can still do your bit even if she does not want to share at the time. It is best to do this when you are having a peaceful moment. Try this for at least twenty minutes each week. Take turns to say:

(i) The things you love about her.
(ii) The things that you would like to be different.
The danger here is to spend too much time on the things you
want to see changed. Make sure you are spending more time at
appreciating.

- Demonstration with two volunteers taking turns to be
  the partner. Usually have some fun doing this exercise.
- Comments, questions.
- Fifteen minutes each way:
  What are the assumptions you make when you say, "I
  love you"?
- Song.
- Feedback to group.
- Speakout.
- Closing circle.

### Session nine: Parenting

As parents we get very little support for the difficult job of
parenting; we are not educated for the role and are expected
somehow to know what to do 'as it comes naturally'. However,
we generally learn how to be parents from the role models
around us and from our own parents. Many of us have been
deeply hurt by the way we were parented and there is a
tendency to pass on these hurts to our own children in turn. It
is important to notice where we were hurt as children so that
we can make a conscious decision not to pass on these hurts in
our own parenting.

Fathers are seen as secondary in parenting, and our role has
been largely to be provider. The recent Child Support Act
reinforces this expectation of men and, coupled with
governmental refusal to support paternity leave, this leaves us
in little doubt about what is expected of us as fathers. One of
the components of men's violence is that we were taught at an
early age that it is acceptable to use violence to gain control of
a situation. Professor Murray A. Straus has studied the effects
of violence on children for over 20 years and he argues that
although violence to children may in the short term produce
conformity; in the long term it will increase the probability of
deviance, including deviance in adolescence and violence
inside and outside the family. The 1975 National Family
Survey in the USA (Straus et al, 1980) showed that over 90 per
cent of families with children aged three and four use violence

on their children. The picture is not much different in Britain. Recently, for example, the Law Lords upheld the right of a childminder to smack a child. Violence breeds violence and if we don't put an end to violence to children, we will always live with violence. We can find other ways of disciplining children and I will explore those with you in the session. Many of us hit children and I want to support you to stop.

- Questions, comments.
- Fifteen minutes each way:
  (i) How were you parented?
  (ii) Similarities you notice with your parenting.
- Song.
- Feedback.
- Group:
  (i) Troubleshooting on parenting.
  (ii) 'Special time' for children.
- Speakout.
- Session.
- Closing circle:
  (i) Something you love about children.
  (ii) Something you look forward to doing with your child or children.

### Session ten: Addictions

The pull to control our feelings and distance ourselves from addictions makes us vulnerable to all kinds of substances and behaviours. As males we are not 'supposed' to feel any pain. Drugs and alcohol serve the purpose of numbing our feelings. Some of you would have been violent under the influence of alcohol or drugs. However, the majority of men who come here would not have been drunk or high at the time of their violence.

It is important that we take some time to look at the way addictions affect our lives and our relationships. As men we are prone to all kinds of addictions, be it drugs, work, tobacco, alcohol, pornography, risk-taking, gambling and so on. Most of these addictions serve the purpose of numbing our true feelings. Often they also affect our health. If we are truly loving ourselves, we would not do harmful things to our bodies or to anyone. So, I encourage you to give up all harmful patterns of behaviour. You would not be in this group now if it was felt that you were addicted to alcohol or drugs; you would have been referred to another agency which specialises in these particular addictions. However, many of us take alcohol at levels that are not good for us. We have a responsibility to look after ourselves well. Let us begin by giving up the addictions that are harmful to us.

- Questions, comments.
- Ten minutes each way on any addictions you notice you may have.
- Song.
- Feedback.
- Group sessions on addictions.
- Speakout.
- Closing circle.

## Session eleven: Goal setting

If we could accurately predict how our lives would be in the future, life would be very boring. However, to live aimlessly without a sense of what we want to achieve can leave us feeling unfulfilled. This means we have to think ahead or have goals. These should be spelled out and specified for every area of our influence and interest. It is best that these goals be flexible, subject to change by intelligent decision and they should not become compulsive. We need goals for ourselves, our families, our communities. We humans have been able to take control over our environment because of our intelligence – here defined as the ability to come up with a fresh answer to any new situation that confronts us. We have done a good job so far, but we have a long way to go to make our environment completely safe for all to live happy lives. Over the past three months we have been working towards the goal of stopping our violence. We started out with a decision to stop and have been working towards this goal by getting support to notice where we have been hurting ourselves, and becoming aware of the society we live in and the role our violence plays.

In setting our goals we have to look far ahead and near at the same time, or our goals could become daydreams. Remember that every journey begins with a single step; in deciding our long range goals it is helpful to work our way back from the goals to whichever first step is necessary. We can have grand goals and more modest short term ones, like taking a child to the cinema next week. If our lives are to be fulfilling it is important that we set goals for ourselves.

- Questions, comments.

- Fifteen minutes each way on goals. To help you set goals a chart is provided.
- Song.
- Feedback.
- Speakout.
- Closing circle.

### Session twelve: Endings

This is the final session in the comparatively short journey we have undertaken in the last three months. We have covered a lot of ground in that time. We have looked at many issues directly related to your violence. At times the issues raised were not so clearly related. I have worked on the assumption that if you are to change your violent behaviour it is necessary to fill the vacuum left with a more caring attitude. I hope the issues we have covered will help you to fill that vacuum. I will recap on the issues we have covered briefly.

It is good that we spend some time saying goodbye to each other. We have shared a lot of ourselves with each other and I have come to know you intimately over that time. I am filled with joy and sadness at the same time. I feel joy that you have completed your sessions here and hope that none of you will repeat your violence. I feel sadness to lose the closeness we have shared. I will now spend a few moments paying attention to each one of you in turn to comment on what I have noticed about you during the time spent here. I will encourage you, in saying goodbye, to do the same for each other.

- Group spends time saying goodbye to each other.
- Ten minutes each way noticing how you feel about ending.
- Song.
- Feedback.

At the beginning I asked that you not meet outside of the group for any reason. I would now like to encourage you to keep in touch with each other, sharing and supporting where you can with the skills you have developed over the time here. For those of you wanting to stay in touch with each other a sheet of paper is provided to put your name and address.

- Questions, comments.
- Ongoing group information for men who feel they need

some more support after completing the course.
- Closing circle.

## References

Hartman, P. and Husband, C. (1974) *Racism and the Mass Media*, London: Davis-Poyntes.

Straus, M. A. (1991) 'Discipline and deviance: Physical punishment of children and violence and other crimes in childhood', *Social Problems*, Vol. 38, No. 2.

Straus, M. A., Gelles, R. and Steinmetz, S. (1980) *Behind Closed Doors*, New York: Anchor Press.

# CHAPTER 7

# WORKING IN THE 'CHANGE' PROGRAMME, PROBATION-BASED GROUPWORK WITH MALE DOMESTIC VIOLENCE OFFENDERS

**David Morran**

### Introduction

The CHANGE Men's Programme came into being as a result of the efforts of a number of individuals who had a general interest in responses being developed for men who were violent to their partners. Among them were several social workers who were concerned that their statutory priorities towards children often meant that they failed to adequately address the needs of women in violent homes, or to confront those men responsible for the violence. Also involved were solicitors and sentencers who were frustrated both at the lack of protection which courts offered women who experienced violence, and at the limited and ineffective range of options available to deal with those offenders who appeared before the bench. Two US academics, Rebecca and Russell Dobash, who had researched and written extensively on domestic violence, and who had been based locally in Scotland for a number of years, lent support and advice and helped steer the group towards examples of good practice existing elsewhere. Additionally, a number of women from different personal and professional backgrounds, some of them associated with Women's Aid, and some with quite mixed feelings about the whole idea of resources being provided to engage with violent and abusive men, also contributed substantially to the discussions and planning which took place.

Work with men who were violent to partners had been going on in the United States and Canada for several years. This had involved a variety of approaches and a wide and sometimes contradictory range of theories as to why men are violent. Generally, there had been no systematic attempt to evaluate what methods seemed to be more or less effective in terms of obtaining positive results. Some men's programmes had, however, won the cautious support of broad sections of the women's movement in the US. These generally combined three basic features. Firstly, they were clear that the men carrying out the violence were the perpetrators and the women experiencing violence were the victims (or survivors). This was a distinction which was sometimes lost in some of the more male-growth orientated therapies. Secondly, these programmes acknowledged the criminal nature of the violence and attempted to work within the criminal justice system. Men's violence was therefore seen as a public, as opposed to a private, issue and consequently violent men could be held accountable by the courts if they failed to comply with the demands or requirements of the programmes they attended. Thirdly, they adopted a pro-feminist perspective, interpreting men's violence not as irrational or dysfunctional, but as behaviour which men employed, intentionally, (if sometimes unknowingly) to exercise power and control, and inflict punishment on women.

These were the guiding principles within CHANGE's steering group. An application for funding to set up a court-mandated programme for male domestic violence offenders and a simultaneous application to evaluate such a programme were separately lodged. In September 1989 the CHANGE Project came into existence, funded through the Urban Aid Programme with the support of Central Region Social Work Department.

### The early phase of the project

CHANGE consisted of three workers, a part time administrator, and two joint co-ordinators, myself and a woman colleague. We worked together as full, equal partners in setting up and running what we would come to call the CHANGE Men's Programme.

The first six months was a time of considerable learning and reflection for me both as a man and as a worker. I had been employed previously as a social worker, dealing mainly with male offenders both in the community and inside prisons. I had often found it frustrating that while the men I worked with were generally very demanding and dependent in their relationships with their women partners, they also expected to be seen as being in charge or in control. In fact, they shrugged off as much personal and emotional responsibility as they could. I was aware, therefore, that I undoubtedly had conflicting motives for wanting to work with men who were violent and abusive. I was looking for an opportunity to 'confront' what I perceived as the shortcomings in other men (many of which I could also recognise in myself). At the same time, I was also aware that most men I had had contact with were in fact not 'powerful' in themselves, but were often confused, isolated, out of touch and uncertain about their roles as men. They needed support as much as confrontation. Unsure of how these views would be regarded within a recently appointed management committee, most of them female, and some with contentious views about what the aims of work with violent male offenders actually ought to be, I was cautious about how I expressed them. However, this tension of working with men to confront them with their violence, as well as to help them in growing and changing as individuals, has been a consistent feature of all the work we have done in this project.

Time was also spent during this early phase reading about examples of good practice, an experience all too rarely afforded practitioners. Of particular importance was the work of the Domestic Abuse Intervention Project (DAIP) in Duluth, Minnesota, which CHANGE staff visited in March 1990. DAIP was significant, not simply because of its reputation concerning the work done there directly with men, but also because of the way that work linked with other necessary 'community co-ordinated' services. These included the provision of women's refuges, and advocacy services for women within civil and criminal courts. There were also policy directives from police, prosecutors and sentencers to deal consistently with domestic violence as an appropriate criminal justice issue. Programmes for men were not seen by Duluth as a 'stand alone' solution for responding to men's violence.

Around this same period, we began to develop the basic elements of our own programme. We started this at a time when the main priority of many local authority social workers had become that of child protection, one consequence of which was a decline in probation standards. Many social workers, (who in Scotland fulfilled the role of probation officers), had become unclear about what their duties were in relation to offenders. Several sentencers had openly expressed a lack of faith or satisfaction with the services on offer. We were all too aware then, as we met with those social workers and sentencers, whose co-operation we needed in developing a pilot project in a comparatively 'new' field, of the need to be **explicit** about what it was we aimed to do, and how we aimed to do it.

### Programme structure

In devising the outline of the programme we needed to ask ourselves not just 'what works?', but 'what works that we, with our limited resources and experience, can sustain?' Of the few research findings on evaluation available to us at that time, one study, (Edleson & Syers, 1985) had demonstrated that relatively short, cognitive behavioural groups of 14-18 weeks' duration were reportedly more effective in terms of stopping men's physical violence over a follow-up period of six months than were other longer, more 'flexible' men's programmes. Consequently, we proceeded to devise a 16-week pilot, which two workers could manage, adapt and refine. This was sustainable and realistic within the terms of a probation order, and would embrace core modules or themes which we could describe to others in comparatively clear language.

### Discussions with social work and courts

From the outset it had been evident from discussions between the Project and the local social work department that the CHANGE programme would operate as a condition of a probation order. Our prototype programme was devised with this format in mind. However, when we came to meet with prosecutors and sentencers, a range of views about how best the programme might function were expressed.

Prosecutors, or procurators fiscal as they are termed in Scotland, considered that work with men might best be done under the auspices of diversion away from prosecution by the court. They were sympathetic to the idea of 'something being done' with men, but foresaw difficulties in this being conducted solely on a post-prosecution basis. They cited cases where they had evidence to prosecute men, but where they felt it had been fruitless to do so. This was primarily because of the nature of the relationship between the victim and her assailant which frequently resulted in a woman dropping a complaint against a partner.

They seemed aware of the pressures and conflicting loyalties which made some women do so and, for the most part, were sympathetic. The prosecution of the man, they argued, often placed even more pressure on the woman because he would plead not guilty. During the time lapse before trial, and despite bail conditions requiring the man to remain apart from the woman, he often did not do so. The pressure on the woman became even greater, or the relationship resumed, and the case came to naught, as did any attempt to engage with the man's behaviour in any personal rather than legal way.

The fiscals argued that if cases could be diverted, or more appropriately deferred from prosecution, then:

a)  the man could be seen speedily and the problem picked up;
b)  he would be given a message that he had to do something about his behaviour or he would be brought back to court, and then prosecuted;
c)  the antagonism which often existed between man and woman when a court date was pending would be absent, thus reducing the tension between them and the pressure which women felt themselves to be under.

We attended these discussions with a pre-determined agenda which was in effect, a condition of Women's Aid's support for any work undertaken with men. CHANGE was thus diametrically opposed to any form of diversion, in view of the fact that domestic violence was criminal, that courts historically had not taken the issue of violence against women seriously, and that men needed to be given a clear message by society that violent behaviour was not to be diverted but was, instead, very much the business of the courts and should be dealt with openly and following public sanction, i.e. prosecution. We were aware of the need to be pragmatic, however, knowing that the fiscals would emphasise the right of the law to decide in the public interest what could and could not be prosecuted, as well as remaining independent from outside interference as to how they should act. At the same time, we knew that if we accepted the terms of diversion we would lose all support from Women's Aid.

We could also see some inconsistencies in the prosecutors' arguments. Principally, if we were to take a man on the basis of diversion, and he failed somehow to comply, then the same pressure on the woman as witness might remain in force. When the man was brought to court he might feel more able to challenge a 'diversion contract' than a probation requirement failure. To prosecute at that stage, after some work had taken place, might only serve to make things worse for the parties, as well as reducing the credibility of our programme. We tactfully acknowledged, therefore, that while we might not be able to offer a service in many of the prosecutable cases they envisaged, we nevertheless did exist to provide a service of sorts. This meant that in cases which freely lent themselves to prosecution then sentencers at least would be able to use our service. The prosecutors agreed.

Our local sentencers have generally been prepared to make use of new or interesting sentencing options. For the most part they were receptive to the idea of an option being available for men who were violent. Although some resented what I think they presumed to be the stridency of our tone, and engaged in discussion over CHANGE's obviously feminist-influenced views as to what underlay men's violence, there was a general willingness to try us out. This was enhanced, I think, by our own recognition of the need to spell out clearly what we proposed to offer, what our criteria for assessment were, and our readiness to undertake our own assessments and provide reports directly to the court. Within six months we began to receive our first referrals for assessment.

### Criteria for assessment

Our criteria for determining men's suitability for the programme have, thus far, remained fairly consistent. We focus on the offence itself, and the context in which it occurred. We attempt to determine with the man whether there might be a pattern to his violence, whether it relates to other forms of behaviour which might also be considered violent or abusive, and whether there seems to be an increase in its frequency or severity. The latter is a crucial factor if one is proposing to work with men who may be continuing to live at home, or who are in regular contact with their partners. We consider the factors which are likely to encourage or motivate him to accept responsibility for his violence and whether he sees any advantage for himself in looking at behaviour he would rather avoid. Is he genuinely committed to attending a programme which he knows will be 'challenging', or is he merely demonstrating interest or remorse to present a reasonable image to the court? We discuss his alcohol and drug use in detail, the stability of his present living circumstances, the quality of his relationship as he perceives it, and whether he is able to comprehend the material likely to be used on the programme.

Ideally, the most important factor in our assessments is the safety of the woman to whom the man has been violent. We determine how her life might be affected if he is considered for a disposal, which leaves him in the community and very often in or around her home. Where possible, we try and obtain her comments in helping us reach a conclusion, although in many cases women opt not to speak with us at this stage. The reasons for this are varied and may be due to fear, coercion, and threats of further retaliation from the man if she discusses things about him he does not want others to hear. Women may also want to keep a distance from contact with professionals out of a concern that they may find themselves blamed for their partners' violence, or out of a desire to minimise the violence in their home, thereby protecting their children from the prying eyes of social workers and their ilk. Their reluctance to talk often compromises our assessment process. Although we may try and clarify what her views are, say through a third party, we are often faced with speaking to the man himself. Therefore we do not hear the more extended and detailed account of his behaviour which the woman (if she feels confident) is likely to provide. We have tried over time to provide support for women in various ways: through contacts at Women's Aid, and through attempts to organise information sessions for partners. This has never proved straightforward. We now ensure that, where women wish, they are informed by regular factsheets about the modules covered by the programme on a week-to-week basis. Women are, however, always made aware, before we even begin working with men, that the programme offers no guarantees. The woman should prioritise her own safety at all times, as well as relying on her own intimate knowledge of her partner to determine whether or not he is changing his behaviour in any way.

## *Men discussing their offences*

Men come up with remarkably similar accounts when asked to explain their violence. They employ several of the excuses used by other offending groups. Alcohol is very often cited as the cause. According to many accounts, this then results in an isolated, uncharacteristic one-off event where the man finds himself 'pushed beyond control' and becomes physically violent. Provocation also features regularly, where the violence is presented as behaviour which may be wrong, but as something which any reasonable man might do in the circumstances. Social workers, both male and female, have sometimes been observed expressing sympathy for men in these apparently 'extreme' situations, and have been accused of colluding with men's accounts (Maynard, 1985). We are aware of the need to guard against such a reaction on our part, knowing that we each bring a variety of subjective meanings as to what constitutes provocative behaviour. Most of these relate, ultimately, to women defying men's expectations as to how they should behave. Provocation by partners can therefore relate to infidelity, or to the failure of a woman to act 'as a normal housewife should' by, for example, not having the tea ready and the kids well-behaved when the man comes home from work. Men expect to be understood when they try and describe these actions. They are surprised to be challenged, and are often irritated that both the court and the interviewer should be making such an apparent fuss.

Most of the men we reject (consistently about one third), we do so due to factors such as 'lack of motivation to look at own behaviour' or 'denial of responsibility.' Even where we have indicated in our assessments that we will not accept men who in our view are too dangerous, it has not necessarily resulted in them facing a higher tariff disposal in the court. There is considerable variation in the way that courts regard domestic violence offenders. Many of the men know this, of course, and for some, opting not to attend our programme may simply mean facing the alternative of a fine.

Where we are satisfied that the man is at least reasonably committed to involvement in CHANGE, he is required to sign an Agreement to Participate. This is the contract between him and the programme which is a condition of his Probation Order.

## Programme content

We have drawn on a number of sources in developing our programme content and have also adapted several cognitive behavioural methods known to be effective in work with other offending groups. CHANGE endeavours to get men to consider their use of violence in detail, building up a picture of each man's pattern of behaviour and exploring situations where he is likely to be potentially violent or aggressive. Participants' values and beliefs about their use of violence are questioned, as are their general attitudes towards and expectations of women. They are encouraged to develop an understanding of the effects of their actions and behaviour by considering the perspective of the other person concerned, and to learn and practise a range of skills in order to help them behave in a non-offending (i.e. non-violent) way in the future.

The programme stresses from the beginning that men are there to look not just at physical violence, but at the other forms of abusive or controlling behaviour which they also employ in order to intimidate, control or punish the women in their lives. Physical violence is often an extreme expression of the way that men think and feel about themselves in relation to women. Merely to stop using physical violence is not sufficient, as these thoughts and feelings will manifest themselves in other subtler ways, usually in the form of psychological abuse. Some women have reported this as being equally, if not more, damaging. We therefore construct a definition of violence which encompasses physical, psychological and sexual forms of abuse. This is helpful inasmuch as it begins to make sense for some men. They have a wider picture of their behaviour as a whole and can see where physical violence fits into the general pattern of the way they behave. For others, however, the breadth of the definition is daunting. It seems to them as though they are being asked virtually to reinvent themselves in the way they behave to their partners. They are very quick to point out the forms of abuse which they feel that their partners mete out to them. They often ask why they are the only ones being called to account, and why women are not involved as they are equally to blame!

This redistribution of responsibility fits closely with the men's own understanding of why they are violent. This is another theme explored in the programme's early stages. As suggested earlier, men commonly explain this behaviour in the form of statements about feeling uncontrollable and inexplicable anger or temper, sometimes exacerbated by alcohol, or as a result of feeling provoked. While CHANGE's position is that women cannot provoke men to violence, our experience has been that to debate this with men at the outset sets up a climate in which no one wins. We have found it expedient and more effective, therefore, not to challenge men on this point of principle. Instead, we move them to accept that women might make them *angry*, but that they have a choice about how they deal with that anger. If we are successful in enabling men to see this, as we often are at this stage, then we can begin to look at situations which appear to escalate into violence or potential violence. We can also enable them to appreciate how their expectations of women, and their sense of themselves as men, results in them frequently being angry, aggressive and often violent.

Most of the men we have dealt with have little understanding of how what they feel affects how they act. From childhood onwards, men are often under pressure to repress feelings and to conform to stereotypes of physical toughness and to be in control or command of themselves and the situations they encounter. It is certainly the case that many of the men going through the CHANGE programme are completely unable to recognise their feelings in most sets of circumstances, feelings which may be quite obvious to the outsider. Instead, they talk of moods suddenly coming over them, as something external and beyond their control. The emotions they do most commonly identify are anger and of being under pressure a lot of the time, afraid that their anger will explode.

One of the first steps we take with the men, some of whom will be living with their partners or at least in regular contact with them, is to explore the circumstances which they describe as provocative or where they are likely to be potentially dangerous. By deconstructing these situations we try to enable men to see that they are conforming to recognisable and recurring patterns of behaviour over which they can in fact have control *of themselves*. In these instances, where men seem to escalate into sudden and apparently inexplicable outbursts, there are invariably a series of cues which they can begin to recognise. These may be words or phrases which they use either to escalate and justify their anger, or which alternatively reinforces their feelings of worthlessness and powerlessness, resulting in them 'needing' to be in control. They may also relate to decisions or choices, for example, to follow or chase a partner, thereby closing off options for her escape. Where men can recognise those early warning signals and they have choice over the way they behave, they can then begin to take responsibility for their violent responses to situations by developing a personal safety plan. This may not affect how men may *feel* in certain situations, but where they recognise that the losses their violence entails outweigh the gains, they are at least capable of recognising conflict situations developing and of choosing not to be violent.

This still leaves men potentially quite dangerous. The ability simply to behave differently if one chooses may be of small comfort to the women with whom these men are in contact. Men also need to face the damaging effects of their violence, and to contrast what they have gained from their violence (power, control, partner in fear) with what they have lost (partnership, trust, affection, respect and self respect).

What we try to get men in our programme to examine are the influences which form their identities as males. These include the expectations which they and others have about themselves, as men, workers, lovers, husbands, fathers, and the expectations which they have, particularly about the women in their lives, and their frequent 'need' to control women, to expect authority and to receive services as of right. This need to be in control, to be right, to be obeyed, while an accurate representation of life for those men who have succeeded in terrorising their families, is (fortunately) in the main, unrealistic but acts, however, as fuel to the flare of anger which is so often present when men are violent. It can only be replaced, or modified, when men see the value not of control, but of equality and partnership in relationships. This clearly involves a re-examination of values which form the core of most of the programme from this point forward. We also develop certain elementary skills, sometimes sadly basic, like the recognition of a partner as a person, for example, and the value of learning to communicate beyond a series of commands and instructions.

Towards the end of their period on the programme, time is spent with the men evaluating where they might be in terms of areas which they still have to work on. These issues are then jointly discussed and agreed and form the basis of much of the men's continuing work with their individual probation officers.

## *Personal observations about working with men*

The men we deal with are invariably white working class Scots
from a scattering of now-defunct mining or foundry towns
common to this part of central Scotland. For the most part,
they appear to conform to fairly rigid stereotypical views
concerning masculinity and the 'natural' role of men and
women. They are often unused to articulating what for others
might be comparatively straightforward ideas or emotions.
They are not infrequently taciturn and, almost without
exception, rebel against what they see initially as a programme
which makes out women to be good, and men bad. A question
most often asked of the workers is, "Why are the women not
here?" Particularly in the early stage of the programme, men
see violence as something which should not have happened,
but also as something aberrant, and usually provoked, in
circumstances which any reasonable man would understand;
not as behaviour which is systematic, controlling or oppressive.
When some begin to realise that their behaviour might be
almost all-pervadingly abusive, they become either very
depressed or very defensive.

It would not be appropriate here for me to go into what all this
means for my female colleague who co-leads the sessions with
me, but I obviously know what it can mean to be a male doing
this work. In brief it is hard, often depressing and quite
isolating. Operating in a culture where there is little tangible
support for men to challenge or change their 'lifestyles', as may
be present in parts of the US, Canada or Australia, can lead to
feelings not only that one is often struggling in the work with
individual men, but that the work itself has little cultural
approval. There is the understandable mistrust of some
women's groups, and an uncertain political climate with little
opportunity for future funding. It is also personally difficult as
a man, where one is often questioning and undermining values
with which one grew up. While it seems relatively
straightforward to 'challenge' men on their violence and abuse,
it is often much harder to know how to respond when they see
much of the conflict in their lives arising from their own pain
and confusion; important life events which may also need to be
heard. There is often a thin line between failing to challenge
men and colluding with them, between listening to them or
dismissing their explanations as excuses. Also, as a male, I am
a constituent part of patriarchy, and patriarchy and all of its
assumptions are under challenge when one engages in this
work.

## The future: Men as offenders or the development of men's work

In reflecting upon the work the CHANGE programme has carried out with men to date, I feel that we have adhered as required to a particular policy position, necessary for the sometimes cautious support of Scottish Women's Aid. That support is conditional on work only taking place with male domestic violence perpetrators providing that they are confronted with the intentionality and criminality behind their violence. Their efforts to shift blame must be resisted, and they must participate in a challenging or demanding course which faces them with the consequences of their behaviour, where sanctions are available in the case of non-compliance. This support is also contingent on any work with men being conducted solely on a post-conviction basis.

In many ways this has felt right. There seems little doubt that by providing a resource which local courts have been able to use, and by offering more options to sentencers, the profile of domestic violence has been raised, its criminality acknowledged, and appropriate disposals or alternatives considered seriously by legal and other institutions whose responses may have been less systematic in the past. It also seems unlikely whether we would have worked with the amount of men we have done, or that we would have functioned in a manner which was so accountable to other agencies, had we proceeded along a diversionary or non-court basis.

Nevertheless, I feel that it is also important to acknowledge that there may be some danger of this kind of work becoming polarised into two camps. Firstly, that which takes place with men on a post-court, 'offender' basis as being supported and somehow worthy. Secondly, that which takes place with men who acknowledge a problem of violence, but who have neither been exposed or prosecuted, as slightly unworthy. The former approach is presently confined to CHANGE and another in-house programme located within Lothian Region Social Work Department, (although some English-based projects are presently in the preliminary stages of partnership arrangements with probation departments). The development of other 'voluntary' or non-statutory work with violent men does, for various reasons, seem to be arising out of what might very loosely be termed the 'men's movement'. Unlike some of the work carried out in the US, which was referred to briefly at the beginning of the chapter, many of these British projects do share a common pro-feminist perspective on male violence. They are attempting to develop approaches to men which are accountable to women and women's experience of violence.

Women's concerns about this largely untested area of practice have to be recognised and taken seriously. While acknowledging these concerns, and their consequent assumptions that only the court-based approach is the way to proceed at present, it is my own personal view that in the near future there is a need for voluntary and statutory programmes for men. Work within a criminal justice setting can publicly highlight the extent, seriousness and criminality of men's violence to women. It can also try to provide constructive and effective resources for those among these men who want to, and seem capable of, stopping their violence. To work *only* in this context, however, necessarily means that only a small proportion of that already small number of men who ever find themselves in the courts for being violent in the first place will be reached. There seems to me to be convincing arguments for the need for some of this same work to be undertaken with the vast majority of men who do not come into contact with the courts, but whose violence and oppression of women partners, and women in general, is just as real.

As Canada and Australia have shown, male domestic violence is the business of the courts and prisons, but it is also the business of family, schools, health centres, workplace, sports centres, community and media. If men are to learn to be non-violent in relationships, then we must start from childhood. Until this ideal can be achieved, programmes for men, whether court ordered or not, merely represent marginal attempts to engage with men who are already violent and who long ago learned how to be dangerous to others. Another concern is that programmes for men will compete for funds with services for women experiencing violence. If this were so, I would certainly share their alarm in full. My own particular anxiety, however, is that while we need to acknowledge women's distrust and even their anger, we as men will become paralysed, for fear of alienating women and their support. Subsequently, we could do no work with these men at all, leaving their violence unchecked and unchallenged. Ironically and paradoxically, those who are committed to attempts to develop services which effectively challenge and stop men's violence against women, may have to face even more of women's anger head-on. This is a bleakly uncomfortable scenario, but one which in the short term may be necessary for a less dangerous and oppressive male culture to begin to grow.

## References

Edleson, J. L. and Syers, M. (1989), 'The Relative Effectiveness of Group Treatments for Men Who Batter' Domestic Abuse Project, Minneapolis MN.

Maynard, M. (1985) 'The response of social workers to domestic violence' in J. Pahl (ed.) *Private Violence and Public Policy*. London: Routlege and Kegan Paul.

# CHAPTER 8

# A PARENTING COURSE FOR YOUNG MEN

## Jane Mardon

### Introduction

Young men in custody. What motivates them to learn, and to change in order to move away from their criminal life style? Is there anything that can bring a spark of enthusiasm to a group of disaffected youngsters who, for the most part, have little or no hope of employment or the opportunity to change their life style? There are ways to motivate and what better motivation is there than becoming a responsible and caring parent? Most of us become parents at some time, and although we had been aware that some young prisoners were in fact fathers, it was late in 1984 that it became apparent that here at Deerbolt Young Offender's Institute (YOI) there were a significant number of them. Officers on duty at visiting times had noticed that many of the inmates had visits from their own children.

Although situated in the N.E. of England in Co. Durham, Deerbolt takes prisoners aged 15-21 years at the time of sentence, from a wide catchment area. These fathers were coming from a large area of the country. Their sentences vary from three months to four years, but because of the time spent on remand and in police cells, the average length of stay is just over 11 weeks. There is a turnover in excess of 1,800 prisoners a year. As so many appeared to be fathers, a question on parenting was added to an induction list used to determine the inmate's needs. In addition to questions there already on homelessness, gambling, drug addiction and many more, a simple question on being a parent was placed on the comprehensive Needs Register. In 1984-85, 30 per cent of all prisoners admitted to being fathers; the percentage is approximately the same today. Of course, the actual numbers may be higher as some do not wish to admit to being parents; usually those who have little or no contact with their child or the mother. As they do not acknowledge their children, it is impossible to know the proportion of inmates at Deerbolt that fall into this category.

The majority of these young men come from poor backgrounds, broken homes and depressed urban areas. A large number of them re-offend but most grow out of a life of crime between the ages of 23-30 years. They often settle down with a wife or partner and children. A significant number are inadequate in some way; they have literacy and numeracy problems, poor social and life skills and frequently a low self-image. In addition, nearly all the men I have taught over the years, do not wish to bring their children up the same way as they were. They definitely want to break the cycle of poor parenting, but find it difficult to know how to change patterns of behaviour.

Many, if not all, of the men have had no experience of a 'preparation for parenthood' course at school. Of course, a great number of them had failed to attend school regularly since they were 12 or 13 years old. Even so, courses offered at school at the time we set up ours, were usually directed at girls and involved the physical side of childcare and development. There have been many changes in schools since 1984 and 'Parenting' is usually now on the curriculum in some form or other. However, the young men coming to Deerbolt do not seem to have attended any of these courses. Some people have suggested that boys are not really interested until they become fathers themselves. This may be just an image they try and put across, for we have recently piloted a shorter course on parenting for inmates at Deerbolt who are not fathers, and it has been extremely well received. Working with young men in a group may well be easier than in a mixed gender setting as perhaps they feel more able to discuss their feelings and sensitive issues, without appearing 'soft' in front of young women.

We felt that the course we wanted to set up should have an equal emphasis on the emotional side of childcare. It should include: looking at joint and individual roles as parents, developing relationships, taking on responsibilities, looking at attitudes, and many other topics such as child abuse and financial pressure on young families.

## The background

In the autumn of 1984 it was reported by officers on duty in the visits room that a large number of inmates were getting visits from partners with young children. The officers were unsure as to whether they were all fathers to the children present, but it appeared that the vast majority were. This was when it was decided to include a question on parenting on the Needs Register questionnaire. Once it was established that roughly a third of inmates were fathers, it was decided that the education department should set up a relevant course for them. Initially the education officer and a full-time member of the teaching staff discussed how this should be organised. It was agreed to invite a representative from the Area Health Authority, a local health visitor who already had an input into the pre-release course, a marriage guidance counsellor (as they were then called) and a part-time teacher who would be responsible for the running and teaching of the course.

There then followed a brainstorming session at Deerbolt which was attended by all the people mentioned above. At this session the modules and their content were decided upon; the input from the health experts proved invaluable. It was decided that I should be the tutor in charge of the course as I was a parent of young children, plus I had a great belief and enthusiasm for this kind of education. In retrospect, the brainstorming session worked extremely well. Although there have been changes in the programme over the years, as explained later on in the chapter, the core of it has remained virtually the same and our overall objectives have not changed. The involvement of a health visitor seemed essential in certain sessions. For the Family Planning session, the health visitor has a particular in-depth knowledge of medical and anatomical terms, experience of dealing with young people at clinics, at schools and colleges and therefore knows the generally acceptable contraceptives for this age group. The Birth of the Baby session was another that seemed to invite an input from the health visitor. The training as both a health visitor and a midwife would provide a specific area of knowledge that would enable her to answer detailed questions. The Child Development sessions were also to involve the health visitor. The topics to be covered on the course were particularly relevant to her role in the community. She could give guidelines in these sessions on how to help a child reach its full potential and stress the importance of the parents' role in a child's development. We also felt that by having her involved in the course, it would help the inmates see that the health visitor is a person to turn to for help, advice and support based on her own experiences.

We also wanted someone from the NSPCC or social services to run the Child Abuse session as their training in discussions of this nature would be essential, especially as it is such a delicate subject – particularly so in a prison environment. In fact, it was this session that we felt needed an input from an expert most of all. At the time, a marriage guidance counsellor attended our induction course talking about relationships. She was happy to work with us on the Parenthood Group, looking at roles, attitudes and relationships.

Finally, we hoped that some of the male members of staff at Deerbolt might be prepared to drop in on the course from time to time to talk about their roles as fathers and their experiences of parenting.

The Parenthood course at Deerbolt thus came into existence in January, 1985 and has been running ever since. It is a modular course which enables the fathers to join at anytime on a roll on/roll off basis. Initially there were ten modules, but over the years, following discussions and evaluation by both staff and inmates, it has changed partly in content and also been extended to 11 weeks. We have eight young men on the course at any one time, they are all volunteers, all parents or about to become parents. Although they do volunteer for the course, it is expected that after the first session they give a commitment to attend all the rest. During the nine and a half years that I have run the course I have only had four inmates ask to leave; two because they had split up with their partners and had found it difficult to cope emotionally with the work we were doing and two because, according to them, they 'knew it all already'. At the end of the course they received a certificate of attendance.

### Course structure

1. Family Planning and Sexually Transmitted Diseases.
2. Birth of the Baby.
3. How a Family Functions – roles, relationships and responsibilities.
4. Child Development 1 – 1st year of a child's life.

5. Child Development 2 – 2nd year of a child's life.
6. Child Development 3 – 3rd and 4th years of a child's life.
7. Child abuse.
8. Outside Childcare and What the State Provides.
9. Health and Safety.
10. Basic First Aid.
11. Visit to the Playgroup.

Most sessions involve the use of test papers, questionnaires, an appropriate video and, most important of all, extensive discussion. The men find the work both challenging and rewarding and the majority of them are extremely well motivated. The group meets once a week for a two and a half hour morning session, rather than everyday for a whole week. This, I believe, is one of the contributory factors to the success of the group, as they rarely lose interest being there for a relatively short period. There is good support for the course from all areas of work in the prison. Officers, instructors and teachers are happy to release their men from work for the weekly session. It was only in the early days of setting up the group that I had a few problems convincing some sceptics of its relevance and worth. Nowadays, the value of good parenting skills is appreciated by the majority of staff. Although there is no specific research on this subject, evidence suggests that parenting and the responsibilities that go with it, if taught successfully could be a way of trying to break the cycle of offending behaviour. So what would be a helpful list of do's and don'ts for someone who is wanting to set up and run a parenting course for men?

**Do's**

1. Plan the course carefully with the help of experts.
2. Constantly evaluate and update the course structure and content.
3. Be prepared for extensive discussion and listen to everyone's point of view.
4. Invite other parents, both men and women, to your group to talk about their roles as parents.
5. Be flexible and keep a sense of humour.
6. Keep to the modular approach so that anyone can join the group at any time.
7. Get help from other people/sources if you feel you need it.
8. Have visiting tutors, who are experts in their field,

involved as much as possible, but ensure that one person is responsible for the course.

9.  Always provide coffee or tea to start with as this helps to create an informal and relaxed atmosphere.

**Don'ts**

1.  Never patronise and never be judgemental.
2.  Don't have the course running all day – keep to short modular sessions.
3.  Don't be afraid to change your programme to fit your client group.
4.  Don't be inflexible.
5.  Don't cancel sessions.

### *Course development*

As previously stated, when the course was first set up, a health visitor used to have an input into five of the modules – Family Planning and Sexually Transmitted Diseases, Birth of the Baby and the three Child Development sessions. A counsellor from Relate helped out with the 'How a Family Functions' module and a representative from Social Services took the Child Abuse session. For various financial reasons and individuals' work briefs, the counsellor and the social services representative departed after a couple of years. Three years ago for similar reasons we were no longer able to have a health visitor working with the group. However, there have been recent developments which involve the participation of staff from Deerbolt's Hospital Group. A nurse/midwife now takes the sessions on Family Planning, Child Abuse and Basic First Aid. The latter session was introduced after the young men decided they wanted a complete module devoted to First Aid, rather than just including it in the Health and Safety session. The hospital staff will also have an input into other sessions as time progresses, probably in the Child Development modules. Their contribution is always excellent and very well received by the inmates. Recently a representative from the DSS has agreed to talk about benefits in Module 8.

As the students on the course have a wide range of ability, questionnaires and test papers are kept relatively simple; the latter testing knowledge acquired during the previous session. These take the form of statements followed by True or False and are enjoyed by all. Questionnaires are designed so that the more literate students can write as much as they wish. All questions on both sheets are read out loud so that their ability to read is not being tested. Those who find it difficult to write down their responses on the questionnaire tend to give their answers verbally when we discuss the individual issues raised. There is always a great deal to discuss. Being apart from their children is obviously very stressful and for some it is the beginning of a realisation that they do not want to spend more time in prison, missing valuable weeks, months and even years away from their families. Nearly all the fathers I have worked with over the years do not wish their children to be brought up as they were. In fact, over the past nine and a half years only a very small percentage has identified their own fathers as their role model. They are often closer to their mothers but frequently saw them being bullied verbally and physically by their fathers or step-fathers. Therefore, they see the mother figure as being weak and subservient to the male. When their mothers have rejected them there appears to be a far deeper hurt than if the father walked out.

Many of the young men have suffered some form of physical abuse at the hands of their fathers or step-fathers. Over the years approximately 70 per cent of the young men on the course have step-fathers. Nearly all of them have poor relationships with their step-fathers; they resent the influence they have over their mothers and they do not like being disciplined by the 'new parent'. Most of them feel they have had poor relationships with their fathers: very little communication between them, no close confiding discussions and little or no emotional outpouring or support. This is not what they want with their own children. They want to be close, to be happy, secure and loving with their children.

To bring out these feelings involves a great deal of soul-searching and openness. We spend a significant amount of time talking about these issues and trying to resolve the problems they pose. Before they can develop the relationships they want with their own sons and daughters, they need to examine their own relationships with their fathers and mothers. They have the same hopes and expectations for their children as all parents do. Because of this they often have a vision of an 'ideal family' as being like the ones portrayed on TV advertisements or across the pages of glossy magazines.

So discussion is absolutely vital to our Parenthood course yet opening up in a very personal way can be extremely difficult for these young men. Talking truthfully about one's feelings is not a general characteristic of prisoners who tend to promote a 'hard macho' image in order to survive in places like Deerbolt. Revealing emotions can bring about ridicule and prisoners tend to keep them to themselves. However, once they identify with the group and the group has worked together for some weeks, many members seem ready to reveal some of their true feelings and ideas and to discuss issues that really concern them as regards their own and their child's upbringing. The group does, in fact, develop a very strong identity and the men support each other in our discussion sessions. It is important not to let just one person dominate discussion work, as inevitably the more confident will tend to talk at length once they have overcome their initial fears of revealing their emotions. Drawing other people into the discussion by asking them to comment on what someone has just said or asking if they agree or disagree, will make sure that everyone gets included. However, some people will always be able to verbalise their emotions more than others. In addition to talking about relationships, we also look at roles, both joint and individual. Many of the young men's fathers have never worked or have had long periods of unemployment. For the majority of the young prisoners there is little or no prospect of work. Some do not wish to work. They have become used to a life living on state benefits, supplemented by the proceeds of crime. The majority would like jobs though and most of them, now that they have children, want to steer away from their criminal activities. They often feel despair at their lack of financial stability and the prospect of long term unemployment. As they have often supported their families and life styles through the proceeds of crime, the prospect of 'going straight' and living on very little is a depressing thought. They do talk about giving up crime in order to be with their children and to set a good example. They do not want to see their own children in prison in the future. They also realise that, in reality, the temptation to provide more than they can afford may become too much and they may well re-offend. They frequently have partners who have part-time jobs and this situation seems quite acceptable to them, although most would not want their partner to have a full time job unless they themselves were also in full employment. Neither are they very willing to undertake part-time work themselves.

Generally the men seem more relaxed about all aspects of child rearing concerning their sons and most would be prepared to do far more with their sons than their daughters. Certainly they are happy to change a wet nappy if it belongs to their son but are less keen if it's their daughter's. They worry about things in the news concerning abuse allegations and frequently raise issues in group sessions about cuddling and kissing daughters. Is it acceptable? What age should it stop? One case in particular, which I recall, concerned a father of 20 years with three daughters, who since his eldest child had started nursery, made sure he always wore his swimming trunks in the bath in case she said anything that might suggest improper behaviour. He is not the only one to have behaved in the same way. It seems to be a real worry to a lot of these young men. Boys too are less of a mystery to them, of course, and they all wait excitedly for the day they will be able to kick a ball round the garden with them.

Most decisions concerning the child such as its health and food are made by the mother, but most arguments seem to arise about discipline. The men tend to be more lenient when the children are younger, but as they get older, discipline, particularly with their sons, frequently becomes harsh and nearly always erratic. We discuss disciplining, temper tantrums, lying, stealing, jealousy, and a wide range of issues. Behavioural problems, in particular, seem to be the cause of much of the conflict in the home. We discuss possible solutions to all these problems. We try to get them to understand that all children are different and therefore what may have worked well for one child won't necessarily work with the next. They are always ready to offer their solutions to the problems, stimulating frequently heated debates when some ideas are rejected by the others. Listening to everyone's points of view is extremely important and it is often through this kind of discussion work that progress is made.

So, there is obviously a great deal of this type of approach and work in our group. There are no such things as professional parents. We rely, usually, on our own upbringing to guide us, but when this upbringing has failed, then what is left? This is why we run our course, to instruct the group members in good parenting skills, to offer help and guidance to these young men; while their chief motivation is love for their child. What exactly do we do on the course? What works well? What are the problem areas? To discover the answers to these questions, the content of the course will now be looked at in depth.

### *The modular structure*

## Module 1 – Family Planning and Sexually Transmitted Diseases

Although the young men obviously have a child or children, the idea of including this session is to make sure that any future children are planned and wanted. It is also to make them aware of all forms of contraception; their knowledge of contraception is surprisingly poor. On each course I hear stories of cling film being used as a condom, Coke being used as a douche and other tales that make your hair stand on end. Leaflets are issued and there follows lengthy discussion on different methods. We also look at whose responsibility *is* contraception. Sexually transmitted diseases are also looked at, at length, and health authority booklets on this topic are distributed. Issues involving abortion always bring about heated debate, for the majority of the young men are very against it in nearly all circumstances. On the initial questionnaire, one of the questions is, "List all the different contraceptives that you know about". The majority have only heard of two: the pill and the condom. This session is usually completed by showing a video. The one currently being used is 'Sex and Drugs and HIV' issued by the Health Development Unit in conjunction with West Yorkshire Probation Service. Sometimes videos are loaned from the local health authority. It is always best to check them before use as it is difficult to find suitable ones for this age group.

This session involves a lot of information giving rather than extensive discussion. The responsibility of contraception is usually seen as a joint one within a stable relationship, however many of the men have sexual relations outside of their regular partner and over the years it appears that condoms are now becoming more acceptable in these casual liaisons, particularly with worries about AIDS. The health visitor used to bring in examples of all the different sorts of contraceptive devices and these were extremely useful. The hospital officer tends to use similar aids plus demonstrating how to put on a condom (using a carrot) as, frequently, the men use them incorrectly. This session is a good one to start with as it involves lots of practical advice, gives plenty of information and doesn't ask them to bare their souls.

## Module 2. Birth of the Baby

The beginning of the child's life is always a popular session.

Those men who have been present at the birth of their baby run riot as they describe the event. To the majority of them it was a wonderful and moving experience. To a few it was a nightmare, particularly if their partner experienced difficulties with the birth. We cover a lot of ground on emotional support for the partner during pregnancy, birth and afterwards. Diet is looked at as well as harmful products such as cigarettes, drugs and alcohol. Generally, the men are not well informed about labour and the changes that occur in the woman's body. There is always a great deal of interest in the growth of the baby in the uterus and in the actual birth. Those who missed the birth of their child, or who will be in prison when the baby is born, often feel quite sad that they are only able to watch birth on video. Those who attended the birth, express their feelings of emotion and what it was like to hold their baby for the first time. Photographs of their children are frequently brought along to this session.

Again, this module is packed with information. There are various videos of the birth of a baby that can be loaned from local health authorities and there is usually a choice for this age group. In addition to the test paper on the previous module and a questionnaire on this one, there are various leaflets from the health authority and information sheets given out. This is often the session when the most difficult medical questions are asked and over the years I have frequently had to ask local nurses for the correct answers.

**Module 3. How a Family Functions**

Most of this session revolves around discussion – looking at joint and individual roles and relationships within the family. It is usually a very productive session although it can be rather slow at times to get going. I usually find it easiest to start at looking at roles in the home by having a pack of cards with various tasks on. The men then sort them out into three piles: definitely a woman's job, definitely a man's and, finally, a joint role. For example, they may see cleaning the car as a definite male role, ironing the clothes as a definite female one, and doing the shopping as a joint one. This is an excellent ice breaking activity, and as the cards are self designed they can include as many or as few jobs as is desired. As rules are constantly changing in today's society, it is interesting to see and hear their views. These young men seem prepared to get involved with many tasks involved not only with child-rearing but around the home too.

It is important to get everyone to join in this initial work as usually it is easier for them to start talking about how roles were defined in their parental home and then for them to progress to discussing their relationships in the past, present and future. The purpose and value of this discussion work has been described earlier. Sometimes if the group's identity is not strongly developed, I will put this session after the Child Development ones. There is always a certain degree of flexibility with some of the modules as to where they actually come in the programme.

**Module 4. Child Development 1**

Here we look at the effect of a new baby on the lives of not only its parents but on the extended family as well. Feeding is looked at in detail, as is post-natal care and development changes. It is a very full session both from a point of view of information and discussion. A second video is shown highlighting a child's development in its first year. It is called 'Baby and Co.' with Miriam Stoppard. Practical work is done in this session too, including making up a bottle feed and sieving cooked chicken, carrots and potatoes and making a purée suitable for a young baby. The purpose of this last activity is to demonstrate how much pleasanter it tastes than a similar tinned variety and how much cheaper it is when you use some of the food that was part of the meal for everyone else. Convenience foods are relatively expensive and certainly after tasting them, the men always prefer the home cooked version!

Many leaflets and information sheets are given out at this session, in addition to the test paper and questionnaire, which is a now familiar part of the course to all members.

**Module 5. Child Development 2**

Although immunisation starts during the first year of a child's life, it is only briefly mentioned in Child Development 1 as that is such a full session. It is dealt with more fully at this point. During this module, temper tantrums are looked at and ways of dealing with them are also considered. There often seems to be little or no discussion between partners about the ways they might discipline their children. They rarely discuss or work out some basic guidelines for generally accepted behaviour. Disciplining just happens when things 'go too far' or 'get out of hand'. Play is also looked at in depth as there are frequently problems in this area. Many men seem to believe that playing with their children involves kicking a ball around, rough and tumble, and watching a video together. Although these are worthwhile activities to do together, they have little knowledge of imaginary and inter-active play and the value of these to a child's physical and emotional development.

## Module 6. Child Development 3

Topics covered in this session include the importance of play and the making of play dough using a simple home recipe. Instructional games are also made during this session, such as picture lotto boards. The men really enjoy making these things and become very involved in the work. We also teach the importance of telling stories to children and reading books. Everyone is encouraged to tell a story out of their heads about something that happened to them as a child. Although some feel reticent about this to start with, most of them can find an anecdote from their past that would be suitable to tell their child. Children really enjoy these true stories and will ask for them to be repeated endlessly. Many books are brought in for them to look at, including nursery rhymes. Most admit to having few books in the home and we aim to encourage them not only to buy more books but to join the local library too. Money that may go on sweets could be saved instead to buy books, and the children's teeth would benefit!

Preparation for schools is also covered during this session. Many of the men have a very anti-school attitude. I try and encourage them to see the teacher as someone who they can work with rather than against and that telling their child, "You do not have to do what the teacher tells you," is not really a very helpful attitude.

Children's infectious diseases are also covered in this session, in addition to the child's general physical and emotional development. Again this is a very full and busy session that involves plenty of information giving, discussion and practical work.

## Module 7. Child Abuse

This is always a difficult and sensitive session regardless of how strong the group's identity is. Even groups that have worked together really well find it hard to discuss this subject. Part of the problem is simply the location. It is prison and offenders involved in any way with offences against children are shunned. It is rarely that anyone would ever admit to wanting to harm his child. However, they are able to discuss the physical abuse that many of them have been exposed to. Over the years, a large majority of the young men on the course have admitted that they have suffered severe smackings, beatings and strappings. For some, this has meant they have ended up hating their fathers or step-fathers or finally attacking their fathers themselves as they became stronger. The majority think that the beatings were acceptable as long as they weren't too harsh and in retrospect they say that they probably deserved it. However, they say that they do not wish to treat their children in the same way. So we look at alternative ways of disciplining and this raises many interesting and practical choices. It is good that they start looking for options that do not involve aggression. In dealing with the physical abuse of babies we usually work through sets of articles from newspapers. We try to imagine what and how situations developed that resulted in a damaged infant, for example, continuous sleep deprivation caused by a crying baby. Most importantly, I tell them that if they ever feel they are going to lose control, to put the baby in its cot, leave the room, even the house, and seek help.

## Module 8. Outside Childcare and What the State Provides

Originally these were two separate modules but as the benefit system changed it was difficult to occupy a whole session on this topic. Nurseries, crèches, playgroups, hospitals, health centres, clinics and schools are looked at in this module. Coping with a child in hospital and visiting the dentist are two important topics. During the second part of the session the amount of money available is looked at and then budgeting. Most of the men have had little or no experience of budgeting and this is an extremely difficult task for them to do. Given that for a number of them their income has been supplemented by the proceeds of crime, they find it difficult to even think about how they could live on the small amounts of money that will be available. We look at the For Sale columns in local papers and imagine buying various baby equipment. We cost it out and then compare it to what it would all cost brand new. It is hoped that they can realise they could make large savings, but unfortunately most of them are very against buying things second hand.

They see themselves, once at home again, wanting to buy lots of things for their children; some say to make up for lost time. I try to put over the view that giving them love, support and attention is far more important. Some of them feel despair at their financial insecurity and admit that they will return to crime in order to provide for their families. They would like full-time jobs but well paid ones that would make it worth their while to come off benefits. Mostly they will not consider part-time work although they are happy for their partners to do it and many say they would look after the baby.

Recently a representative from the DSS has started to come in and work with the group on budgeting to explain all the benefits, including the Family Credit system. Budgeting is a vital skill to learn and one that may well help them to stop offending in the future, given that they do indicate they are keen to stop crime now they are fathers.

**Module 9. Health and Safety**

This is an extremely popular session based round the 'Play it Safe' booklet issued by the health authority. All aspects are covered at all the age ranges and I'm sure all the young men will make certain they have a smoke alarm installed when they leave Deerbolt! Leaflets and information booklets are distributed.

**Module 10. Basic First Aid**

This relatively new session is taken by one of the Hospital Group and covers most aspects of a basic first aid course: breathing, burns and breaks. In addition to theory, it is also a practical session, using a resuscitation doll and learning the many uses of a triangular bandage. This is also a very popular session and was introduced at the instigation of the men themselves.

**Module 11. Visit to the Playgroup**

As we run five courses a year, there are five visits to the playgroup. For various reasons at the moment it is not possible to visit more frequently, but it is such a worthwhile and relevant activity that I hope things will change in the future. Two men from each course are chosen to visit. They must have their 'outable status', which means they can leave the prison for periods of work, for visits and home and probation leave.

Only two go rather than the whole group, as they should participate rather than observe. Having just two extra people at the playgroup means that they work and interact with the children. They have a questionnaire to fill in on their return, including a free page for comments. I have included one young man's views at the end. Without exception they really enjoy their mornings with the children. Initially they are lacking in confidence, but as soon as they are seated at one of the activities tables and the children involve them in what they are doing, they immediately forget any qualms they may have had. The visits are extremely successful. They learn a great deal about play including making works of art from egg cartons and cereal packets!

## Feedback

### My Visit

I visited the playgroup in Barnard Castle today. John went too. It was strange walking through the town as I thought everyone was looking at us in our prison gear. When we got to the hall we met Jenny, who is the playgroup leader, and Jill who helps her. They were very friendly and chatted to us about what we were going to do. Then the children came in. Some of their Mums stayed but most left them there for all the morning. There was one Dad who stayed. First I was on the play dough table and I helped Kirsty and Helen to make shapes with it. It was great. We talked a lot and Helen said she knew me but she didn't. Then I did some finger painting with Jonathan and Ben. They were lively and kept going off on trikes. Sometimes they went too fast and got real noisy, so Jill had to stop them riding about.

After that I read a story about the Gingerbread Man. Then we had a cup of coffee and the children had milk, orange juice and crisps. Later we made engines out of boxes, silver foil and cotton reels and other stuff. They really liked doing this. We helped clear up at the end and put the slide, sandpit and water away. I really enjoyed the morning and playing with the children. I learnt a lot about what goes on at a playgroup and it gave me some ideas about things to do when I go home in 6 weeks. My baby is only 18 months old so she won't be going to playgroup yet. I'd like to say thanks for taking me.

**Evaluation**

It is very difficult to evaluate the success of the Parenting course. The majority of young men who attend it do not come back to Deerbolt although they may well re-offend and go to other institutions. They rarely write to let us know how they are coping with fatherhood. Home Office research has shown that they do learn new skills in dealing with children and that their attitudes change after they complete the courses (Caddle, 1991). Our course's success is measured in several ways. One is the demand for it – there is always a waiting list of participants and there is a negligible drop-out rate. Given that these young prisoners often find it difficult to stick at anything with enthusiasm and motivation for very long, it is always a pleasure to see how keen they are to attend every week. They build up a portfolio of their work, their leaflets and information sheets, and take these with them when they leave.

Another indicator of success is the fact that they frequently tell me that they discuss their child/children more with their partners at visiting times, including problems that might arise. They are also keen to impart their newly acquired knowledge to their partners, although at times some of them have said their partners get cross if they show they know more than them!

The skills of parenting have to be taken seriously and I believe the young men at Deerbolt begin to see this and will build on what they have learnt here. I am hopeful of change in their attitudes and a greater understanding of the needs of their children. Even if they acquire only some new skills or retain a few ideas, it is progress and at least the seeds have been sown for change. Being in prison and apart from their children is hard for them. They are keen to be good parents and to break the cycle of poor or inadequate parenting. At Deerbolt we believe we give them some hope of this.

## My Views on the Parenthood Group

I joined the Deerbolt Parenthood Group about 10 weeks ago. It covers many aspects and makes you think about what it means to be a father. I think it is a very good course for young prisoners as not only does it help you catch up on things you are missing, it also teaches you about safety and about relationships. I had a terrible relationship with my father and even now I don't want to ever see him again. I don't want my baby to feel like that about me. The course helps you to handle things like that. We all talk about it and everybody gives their ideas. It's good. It's helpful. It also teaches you about changes in your wife or girlfriend throughout pregnancy and after the birth. It shows you how your partner can get stressed or depressed coping with the child's needs. It really gives you the view that you should share the responsibility of bringing up your child and not just by doing the shopping and cooking. While I've been on the course I've been involved in group discussions with the television. This shows the outside world how hard it is for us to be in here missing our children and it's made us realise that it is important for us to be there for them and not to be inside. Without us around, our children's upbringing will be affected.

### References

Caddle, D. (1991) 'Parenthood Training for Young Offenders: an evaluation of courses in young offender institutions', *Research and Planning Unit Paper 63*, London: Home Office.

# CHAPTER 9

# THE ROLE OF TRAINING IN THE DEVELOPMENT OF WORK WITH MEN

**Trefor Lloyd**

### *Introduction*

I have worked with men for more than 20 years. It was in the mid-70s, when working as a social worker in a men's lodging house, that I began to find it increasingly difficult to ignore the common themes I was seeing amongst the men I was working with. This was in spite of the strength of 'individualist' casework theory that was so dominant at the time.

There are common themes, such as men without work finding it difficult to have an identity; men losing work through illness (and vice versa); men drinking excessively and finding it difficult to get purpose in their lives. These men were individuals, but the form and nature of their 'problems' had a lot of similarity. Since that time, virtually all of my work has been with men (apart from – some may think ironically – three years of working with women with drink problems). The settings have changed from social work, to youth work, and more recently in schools, youth clubs, health and probation. But men, or more accurately masculinity, has been the common theme.

Over the years, as levels of awareness of gender, sexism and more recently masculinity have risen, training has become an increasingly large component of this work. It is the function and role of training that this chapter aims to concentrate on, although training's contribution to the development of working with men will also be explored. I have based this chapter on the

work of Working with Men and The B Team[1] (the two agencies
I work for) and from observations of, and discussions with,
practitioners trying to develop their work with men around the
issues of masculinity and sexism.

## Training as a solution

Picture this: we are in a large voluntary agency, there is a staff
meeting in progress, workers from a number of units are
present. One of the workers raises the issue of violence. She
says that within her unit the men are very boisterous and in the
last few weeks this has spilt over into three fights and she is
concerned. Other workers nod in agreement, they have been
experiencing the same thing. Another worker asks about what
is provoking these incidents? As the animated conversation
unfolds, it becomes apparent that maybe violence is only part
of the issues at play. Workers' confidence of dealing with
violence, some men's (and it is established that it is on the
whole men) near violent ways of communicating, and the
impact of this on other men all make up the 'problem'. After
some discussion, the chair of the meeting, in an attempt to
move down the agenda, asks what workers want to do about it.
Two minutes later, someone has been given the responsibility
to find a trainer to offer a course on 'men, masculinity and
violence'.

Maybe with reduced budgets for training and staff cuts, the
scenario above is rarer than it once was, but the point is to
highlight how quickly we turn to training as our solution to
what is a much more complex problem. Particularly in areas
such as non-discriminatory practice, equal opportunities,
racism, sexism and heterosexism; where knowledge, attitudes
and behaviours, individual and societal aspects, policy and
practice, all play an important part, we seem to turn to training
for some insight, direction and solutions to these seemingly
intractable problems. Of course, this has caused problems of
its own; the questioning of the value of 'racism awareness
training' is, in part, a critique of training's role in the
development of practice and change (Gurnah, 1983).

In spite of this critique, training is still looked on, by many, as a
panacea for insight, awareness, skills and the confidence to
make us better workers, able to impact more effectively and
communicate this knowledge to our colleagues.

Training is of course a very important aspect in enabling workers' practice to develop in areas that have a very short history, such as work with men and masculinity. However, it is also important to ensure that training is in its appropriate place, which also means ensuring that our expectations of training are realistic and achievable, and of relevance to the issues we want addressing.

Currently, in the rapidly growing areas of men and masculinity work, we are short of clarity about the function and role training can take. A number of assumptions, styles and ways of working have developed. Should the training be for men only? Should the trainer be male? Should the trainer be female? Should it be about masculinity or about anti-sexism – are these indeed the same? These and many others are questions and positions that workers have taken in both the development of the work and of training. Too easily, we can become distracted by methods and ideology, and allow these to dictate practice and training; as if the work is not complex enough!

### Masculinity and the youth service

To illustrate some of these issues, I want to look at the way that work around masculinity has developed within the youth service. By 1980, much of the theoretical and practical framework of 'girlswork' had been established; there was a very active and respected 'Girlswork Unit' at the National Association of Youth Clubs. While resistance to this work was strong, female youth workers were developing provision for young women (often separately through 'girls' nights') with some areas very well established and supported at a youth worker level (Young, 1985).

Along with these developments, came a reaction from some of the boys. 'Mooning' at windows, large groups gathering outside of youth provision and even 'picket lines', particularly during the miners' strike, were regularly reported. These reactions sometimes intimidated the girls, and indeed female workers, and sometimes made them even more determined to have opportunities without the boys around. Female workers began to ask, even demand, that male youth workers, "do something with the boys". Sometimes this meant, "Get them out of the way, so we can get on with our business", at other times this meant "Challenge their sexism". Some male workers took up the challenge. This sometimes led to confrontation outside clubs, young men getting 'treats' for being disruptive, such as being taken out on girls' night. Sometimes there were discussions about sexism, young men's own desire for 'space', and even about masculinity.

The bottom line of this work was to stop the boys from disrupting the girls, and anything over and above this was seen as a bonus. In hindsight, it is clear that the focus of this work was the young women and not the young men. Its starting points were the protection of young women and workers, and the reduction of disruption within the youth club environment.

For many male workers, the practice often separated them from the young men who were resisting or responding with such comments as, "Not all this again". While there was a recognition that challenging sexism was very important, there was also the realisation that it wasn't a useful point of entry; that challenging young men about the needs of young women left them resistant, sometimes confused and often resentful.

An approach that acknowledged young men's experience began to develop. This placed an understanding of masculinity at its centre and was seen as both a useful point of entry, because it addressed the issues as they affected the young men, as well as having important contents. Workers began to form usually small groups of young men, where the content of discussions was masculinity (the process of growing up as men) and young men's experience and understanding of it.

Tension began to develop between the two approaches. There was suspicion of boyswork for not addressing sexism through challenge, but simply letting the young men off the hook. While the anti-sexist approach was criticised for its non-workability and just an opportunity, for some male workers in particular, to verbally beat up young men.

These tensions reflected quite different views of what the work was aiming to do, and whose benefit it was there for, and it still pervades **most areas** of developing work with men. Within domestic violence projects, for example, these tensions exist, but at least in most projects and initiatives the assumptions and aims are clearer.

## Domestic Violence Intervention Project

DVIP (Domestic Violence Intervention Project) describes itself as an organisation that places women's and children's safety first and believes that men 'should be accountable for their behaviour'. This has quite different implications from the Everyman's aims which are primarily about, "Stopping male physical and sexual violence", and "to enable men to examine and re-evaluate their attitudes to masculinity, sexuality, relationships and violent behaviour" (Lees and Lloyd, 1994).

DVIP could be described as an anti-sexist project and the Everyman as one within the boyswork (masculinity) mould. Each has its own place. Problems arise where there is a lack of clarity about purpose, aims and outcomes. Especially where multi-agency work has developed, different views of purpose, aims and approaches have caused tussles and arguments because of this tension. It occurs particularly over whether the main focus of the work is protection of women and children or the violent men themselves. In some areas of work and training there is a lack of clarity, in fact, some terms and concepts are used interchangeably. Anti-sexist, masculinity, sexuality, and gender are thought to be very similar concepts, rather than different but overlapping ones.

This has been a very important area for training. Understanding of terms, concepts and perspectives sits squarely within the training remit, but also within management and strategic development. Here lies one of our barriers: management do not necessarily understand the concepts or have the clarity of purpose, any more than workers. On the whole, initiatives in probation, youth work, health and schools come from fieldworkers and not management. So, if workers cannot turn to management and planners, then where do they turn? Rightly or wrongly they tend to turn to training.

## The focus of training

One of the messier dilemmas that has arisen within boyswork and the youth service has been the focus of the training. Is it on self-awareness and personal development, "Until I am sorted out how can I do the work?" Is it theoretical and ideological knowledge and awareness, "Where does patriarchy come from", and, "We have to understand sexism, racism, heterosexism and the rest, before we can do the work"? Or is it practice steps and curriculum ideas "Where do I start to do a piece of work", or "Give me some ideas of what I could do"?

Personally, I have found myself offering training from each of these different perspectives, thinking at the time that they would all result in the development of good practice with men. Many of the early training courses I ran were purposely focused on personal development, on the assumption that if workers were encouraged to talk openly about themselves as men, and about the tensions that they themselves had experienced, then this would equip them to go out and offer this to other men. What in fact happened was that the courses, on the whole, went very well, but workers were reluctant to develop pieces of work.

When I followed up course participants, some said how much they benefited from the course; how their level of awareness about masculinity and gender had risen, but that they had also realised how much there was to know and said they thought they needed a follow-up course. Where others had tried to develop pieces of work, they had consciously, or otherwise, tried to recreate the training course environment, where they had felt safe and able to express themselves. This sometimes led to disastrous results with men becoming very resistant or even aggressive, feeling manipulated by the process. This was mainly because the worker had not taken into account the starting points of the men they were working with. This led to a de-skilling of the workers, too often leaving them thinking that this was very important work to develop, but that maybe they were not up to it.

## Theory and ideology

Theory and ideology have littered work with men and not always in a helpful way. Ideology has contributed to many of the 'shoulds...' that exist in some workers' minds. "Groups should be boys-only", "We should have male leaders", and "We should challenge the boys from the start, not let them get away with anything", are all too common viewpoints, either voiced or just under the surface. These statements are usually rooted in an ideological perspective about men that often interferes with workers being able to respond to what men need. These ideological perspectives usually have at their base something akin to: Men are bad, "If you give them an inch, they will take a mile", "Men only change if under pressure", and "There has to be an element of punishment, otherwise how will they know what they have done is wrong?" Reflections on these perspectives are again an important part of the training function. Some trainers have encouraged workers to use these 'positions' as tenets of the work, rather than perspectives that need to be reviewed, to ensure that they do not become barriers to the development of work. Some men do need to be 'pressured' and a lot of men do need a tight structure and boundaries, but not all, and a skilled trainer notices those that do and those that don't.

While ideology and theory have their place in the development of working with men; methods, approaches and styles need to be determined by what we are trying to do. So, for example, if we are wanting to encourage men to reflect on being men, and we judge that they will do this if we meet away from their area with a female worker that they trust, then this is what we try to do. Pragmatism, and ensuring that we achieve our purpose, come before rigid ideology.

### Training practice

Over the years, Working With Men's training has developed a very strong 'practice' orientation. This has come about because our training aims to equip workers to develop their work with men. We are primarily concerned with what workers do as a result of the training and not levels of personal development. Clarity about our purpose has led us to offer training that impacts on workers' practice, rather than how much they learn; how enthusiastic they are about the training course or how well participants get on with each other. Our interest in course process is much lower than in participants' confidence, willingness and enthusiasm for developing work, and their ability to put this into practice.

This practice orientation has seen the content focus on participants' understanding of masculinity; their grappling with the impact masculinity has on men (especially within a groupwork environment) and strategies and practice steps for participants to consider when developing their work. The courses have 'personal development' content; they have a number of 'basic assumptions' about men, but these are secondary to enabling workers to develop their practice with men.

### Literature about men and masculinity

Returning to the training remit, another aspect of working with men that has resulted in training taking an excessive burden, is the lack of practical literature being generated. Over the last five years a steady stream of books about men and masculinity have been published in the USA, Australia and here in Britain. These have included Bob Connell's exploration of knowledge and politics; Vic Seidler's investigation of social policy and philosophy; Robert Bly's look at mythopoetic man; Christopher Kilmartin's review of current literature; Neil Lyndon's attack on feminism and some feminists; Jeff Hearn's look at organisations and Geoff Dench's alternative look at patriarchy (Bly, 1990; Connell, 1995; Dench, 1994; Hearn, 1992; Kilmartin, 1994; Seidler, 1994). And these are the generalists! I could list another grouping of writers about violence; sexuality; sexual abuse; power; relationships with men; relationships with women and many more, but how much do these contribute to the practitioners' ability to do the work?

Some of us are inspired by the abstract, the indirect, theory, books we completely disagree with. The literature is expected to carry a similar burden to training, much more than it deserves. Literature with a focus on practice is sparse. This is, in part, because publishers do not believe that welfare books about practice sell (Salond, 1993) and also, in part, that practitioners so often say they are too busy doing the work to write about it. So where do practitioners turn to but training!

This book is a rarity, in that it describes examples of practice written by practitioners. Books such as this will help to readjust the balance in the literature. The focus of this book is also on the criminal justice system and the development of work that is informed by an understanding of masculinity and offending. It is to this that we will now turn.

### Masculinity and offending

Training has already impacted on work with men in this area of development. Working With Men has been offering training within probation for over four years and supported a number of initiatives within criminal justice work. Most of the issues mentioned above impact, inhibit and sometimes severely disrupt, developing work.

The surprise about masculinity and offending work, especially within the probation services, is that it hasn't been developed before, or maybe it has! With such a high proportion of men in prisons, on probation, in trouble, the link between men and offending has been taken as a fact which is so fundamental that it does not require questioning. As in most other work areas, it was the awareness of gender, through women and offending as a result of feminism, that provided the platform for a conscious questioning about the link between masculinity and offending. It is the conscious awareness of masculinity that is relatively new, as practitioners have developed practice with men and developed methods and styles that have taken into account that those they work with are in fact men.

### Masculinity and discrimination

The work in this volume has developed out of a conscious consideration of masculinity, although the tensions between masculinity and sexism and anti-discriminatory practice, coupled with questions about who the work is supposed to benefit, links with a whole series of already-existing tensions around other work. Is probation punishment or help? Should probationers enjoy themselves? What balance should there be between 'work' and 'treats'? These are all familiar tensions. Similar difficulties beset work in the areas of masculinity and anti-sexism. Do we continue to see men as perpetrators or does this new awareness now mean that we see men as victims? This is the same question whether we focus on masculinity or sexism. Do men now become the new victims? If they do, does that mean women become the perpetrators?

This 'good guys/bad guys' mentality highlights our too often one-dimensional theory and practice base, especially within the area of anti-discriminatory practice. Within training courses, participants find themselves trying to decide who has 'more power', a black man or a white woman, or which is more important, racism or sexism. It becomes apparent how difficult, given our current theory-base, it is to deal with more than one dimension at a time. Course participants will make comments such as, "If we acknowledge that men are forced into particular ways of being men, then we have to view them as victims and then what happens to women? The bloke hits a woman, but he does it because he was trying to prove himself a man. Where does that leave women?" Or, "Black men may be sexist, but it is because of racism, which is more important to deal with".

These comments reflect either an inability or an unwillingness to look at complex issues. If, like Farrell (1993), we decide that because men are seen as not being able to look after children, and that it is natural that men die earlier than women, then this constitutes sexism. Consequently, sexism becomes two way traffic between men and women, then we are down the one-dimensional path. Similarly, debates about men who sexually abuse, too often stop at describing them as monsters and blaming them for their actions. Whereas women who sexually abuse are more likely to be seen as victims of previous traumas. This again reflects a one-dimensional view of men as bad and in need of punishment, while women are good and have good reason for their behaviour.

This is, I believe, one of the most important training tasks. It can enable practitioners to grapple with the complexity of an issue, whilst not freezing them into inactivity – which often results from practitioners being overwhelmed by that complexity. Models will have to develop that engage and deal with differences between societal and personal responsibility. This will result in creating choices for men and dealing with both the way that men experience masculinity and behave in sexist ways. It will avoid individual men saying, "I am just a product of my environment", or, "I had no choice". These are issues with which most criminal justice workers are already familiar. Training can contribute to understanding the complexity of the issues, but can't be burdened with strategy, direction and wider contextual issues as has been the danger in other professional areas.

### Course components

Courses have four inter-related components:

1. An opportunity for participants to reflect on their own experience of being men by reacting to a simple model of masculinity.
2. Participants using this model look at the impact that masculinity has on the men that they work with and particularly on their offending behaviour.

3.    A series of practice components that are suggested to participants as implications of masculintiy. These tend to stimulate participants to reflect and think about their practice.
4.    The course ends with an opportunity for participants to plan how they will use what they have learnt in their practice in the short term.

### Focus on masculinity

A question that has arisen within masculinity and offending, has been whether a masculinity focus is an end in itself or a means to other ends. Within a day centre in Northern Ireland and a London prison, short programmes have been offered to men at an assessment stage. These seem to have enabled individual men to identify their learning needs. Through the course content, an environment has been created that has given individual men the opportunity to reflect on broader needs and the confidence in themselves to articulate them. This focus on 'process' may have enormous potential in general work with men as a needs analysis tool, as it seems to break down the barriers so common within probation and criminal justice environments.

At such an early stage of development it is difficult to say where the major contribution will be made by an understanding and focus on masculinity within criminal justice work. With developments in assessment work, as an underlying series of principles (as within a lot of domestic violence initiatives) or an overt series of sessions, it may be in any one of these three, or all of them, although in the short-term there is an important role in monitoring and reflecting these developments, which can't fall within the training brief!

### Conclusion

Within this chapter it has been suggested that the role of training in the development of working with men around issues of masculinity and sexism has been overinflated. This has, in part, been a result of management's lack of understanding and direction in this work, as well as a dearth of literature that tackles practice issues, leaving workers having to use training to compensate for the lack of other options.

The need for clarity in terms, understandings, approaches and, most importantly, in what is our purpose in developing this work, is essential. Whether training has a personal development, ideological or a practice-based focus is dependent on the outcomes required from the training; and a practice-based focus is more likely to raise practitioners' confidence and enable them to develop pieces of work. However, as I have suggested, this itself is not unproblematic.

Where masculinity and offending initiatives fit within the broader framework of anti-discriminatory practice will need some careful consideration, as will the need for more complex and sophisticated models of understanding and praxis. At this time anti-sexism approaches fit neatly within the current framework, but a masculinity-focused approach does not.

Unless management, publishing houses, and strategic planners take up their appropriate role within this emerging work area, then training and trainers will continue to be overburdened with an unrealistic role for the future. This is not in the best interests of the work.

## References

Bly, R. (1990) *Iron John*, Harmondsworth: Penguin.

Connell, R. W. (1995) *Masculinities*. Cambridge: Polity Press.

Dench, G. (1994) *The Frog, The Prince and the Problem of Men*. London: Neanderthal Books.

Farrell, W. (1993) *The Myth of Male Power*. London: Fourth Estate.

Gurnah, A. (1983) 'The politics of racism awareness training'. *Critical Social Policy*. Spring.

Hearn, J. (1992) *Men in the Public Eye*. London: Routledge.

Kilmartin, C. (1994) *The Masculine Self*. Basingstoke: Macmillan.

Lees, J. and Lloyd, T. (1994) *Working with men who batter their partners: An introductory text*. London: Working With Men/The B Team.

Lyndon, N. (1992) *No More Sex War: the failures of feminism*. London: Mandarin.

Salond, I. (1993) 'Book Publishing and the Academic Trend', *Working With Men*, 1993:3.

Seidler, V. (1994) *Unreasonable Men: masculinity and social theory*. London: Routledge.

Young, K. (1985) *The Readers' Routemap*. Leicester: National Youth Bureau. (Now the National Youth Agency.)

## Notes

1.  *Working With Men* produces a quarterly journal for anyone working with men around the issues of masculinity, sexism, violence, sexual abuse and education. Each issue reflects developing practice in schools, youth work, health services and criminal justice. Working With Men also provides training and consultance in all of these areas. *The B Team* develops, produces and sells resources (games, posters, packs and other publications) to aid the development of work with men.